Aut[illegible]ted

THE Automated Office

An essential guide for Managers

Stephen Morris

Heinemann Professional Publishing Ltd
22 Bedford Square, London WC1B 3HH

LONDON MELBOURNE AUCKLAND

First published 1988

British Library Cataloguing in Publication Data
Morris, Stephen, 1955, Nov. 14 –
The automated office:
an essential guide for managers.
1. Office practices. Automation. Management
I. Title
651

ISBN 0 434 91069 4

Typeset by JCA Typesetting, Ringwood
Printed and bound in Great Britain by Dotesios Printers Ltd,
Bradford-on-Avon, Wiltshire

Contents

Preface

The efficient handling of information is the staple diet of most businesses today and the volume of information that most of us need to handle seems to increase almost daily. At the same time the world appears to be shrinking fast as it is encircled by more and more communications links. This creates exciting prospects for the future. The idea that any item of information, whether a standard text document, a graphic illustration or a combination of the two, can be whisked around the world in a matter of seconds, revolutionises our view of communications – and yet many aspects are already here.

However, there is an inherent danger in not being able to cope with the sheer volume of information that is becoming available to us all. To succeed, any business or organisation needs to be in tight control of its flow of information.

The aim of this book is to introduce the person, new to all or some of the modern office technologies, to the facilities offered by the equipment and the features you may expect to find.

In all branches of office automation there is an extensive range of equipment from numerous suppliers and manufacturers. It is impossible to list even a reasonable proportion of the market.

Throughout the book examples are given of just a few of the alternatives available. This does not mean that those mentioned are necessarily highly recommended or that they are streets ahead of their competitors. Inevitably, the ultimate choice for any office will depend upon its specific needs and the constraints placed upon its manager. The equipment mentioned, while worthy of investigation, should be only a part of the range considered.

It is hoped that the descriptions given and the examples that are included will sufficiently whet the appetite of readers so that they will be keen to take an interest in the fascinating and ever-changing world of office automation.

Chapter 1

The office automation environment

Office automation equipment

Quite how *office automation* is defined is largely a matter of personal preference. Certainly one must include computers, their programs and peripheral devices. This gives a good start because any equipment that can be connected to a computer immediately offers itself as a suitable candidate. However, some selection criteria are obviously necessary to cut down the topic area. Facsimile machines, digital telephones and dedicated word processors are clearly to be included; yet robots used in car manufacture, air traffic control equipment and microprocessor-controlled toasters seem rather too remote from the office to be considered under that title, although they certainly use the same technologies. Their aim, as with that of the office automation products, is to perform traditional tasks faster, more efficiently and with a greater degree of success. (And it certainly seems to be true that many computerised toasters burn the toast just as efficiently as their mechanical counterparts!)

However, although the majority of office automation products are based on computer technology or are linked with it in some way, this is not the whole story. Photocopiers, for example, are an integral part of many offices and a vital link in the information chain.

For the purposes of this book the term *office automation* is taken to include any equipment that enhances the flow of information within an office and the communication of that information to the outside world. Inevitably there will be omissions, but most branches of office automation are covered in one way or another.

Computers and software

The centre of the automated office is inevitably the computer. This does not mean that every office must have a computer in order to be regarded as modern and efficient; indeed in many small businesses in particular the costs of computerisation often outweigh the benefits.

The computer is the means by which most information can actually be stored and, once entered onto the system, can be manipulated to produce the results you are seeking. Of course, storing information on a computer does not of itself solve any problems. The information (now transformed into 'data') can be inspected and thus saves on storage space. But you need to do something with it to receive the benefits of the time and effort spent getting it there.

This is the task of the *software*, the programs that are used by the computer to perform some specific operation. There is a massive range of programs dedicated to performing individual jobs: *word processors* to manipulate text into letters and reports; *databases* to swallow information and regurgitate it in endless sorted lists, selections and permutations; *spreadsheets* to take last year's results and project them into a plan for this year; accounts programs to take the raw data of our accounts information and transform it into sales and purchase ledgers, trial balances, customer statements and VAT returns.

Added to this there is a range of *service software* whose sole task is to make the operation of the computer more effective in some way.

There is *communications software* to help you communicate with others and you can write your own programs if none of those available suit your needs - or pay someone else to do it for you.

Finally, there is the *integrated software*, that breed of program suites that aim to bring together the disparate strands of data manipulation into a single collection of information. It is here that the potential for the information revolution really begins to become apparent.

Other office automation equipment

There is much more to office automation than putting a computer on your desk. The transfer of information is of crucial importance, but it cannot always be done by computer and the computer is not always the most satisfactory means anyway. Photocopiers play an important part in duplicating sheets of information and facsimile machines transmit these same sheets to other users.

Voice communications have a long way to go before they are ready to be fully

A VIENNA office: the floor-standing shared-resource computer in the centre foreground supports the department's terminal devices, three displays and one letter-quality printer

integrated into the world of computers and yet major advances have been made in the equipment that is available. Telex machines still provide an ideal medium for the transfer of written messages while dictation equipment supplies the means to store the spoken word for future use.

Other devices, such as radio pagers, electronic typewriters and telephone answering machines all have a role to play in the automated office. The task of the manager is to select the right equipment for the job at a price he can afford.

However, the role of the office automation manager goes much further than this. It is also his task to ensure that the installation of the new equipment is carried out smoothly and with the minimum of disturbance to normal office routines. This means that a certain amount of preparatory work must be done. If the accounting staff walk into the office one morning and discover that their adding machines and typewriters have been replaced overnight by brand new computers and accounts programs, as yet unwrapped, the transition is unlikely to be trouble-free!

The manager is thus responsible for all the necessary groundwork to pave the way:

- Adequate consultations with those who must operate the new equipment to ensure that they are happy with it.

- Training so that they can learn the skills and familiarise themselves with the new concepts before the machines arrive.

- A period of dual operation, when the old and the new operate side by side, to iron out any difficulties and provide a check on accuracy.

All this means that the manager must budget for more than just money. That other scarce resource, time, must also be carefully allocated in sufficient quantity if the period of implementation is to be a success.

Once the first few steps down the office automation road have been successfully taken, life becomes a little easier but there are still decisions to be taken. The materials needed to keep the equipment running must be in constant supply. Updated equipment must be planned well in advance. And then, of course, there's always the question: What, if anything, should we automate next?

With the office automation scene constantly shifting there is no doubt that the decisions will never be easy, there will always be plenty to do and the passage forwards will certainly not always be smooth, but the next few years are going to be an exciting and interesting time for all those involved in the development of the office.

Why automate?

The first question anyone should ask before installing any new piece of equipment or updating existing systems is: Why? It is far too easy to get on the office automation treadmill and to feel that you are failing in your duties if the office is not constantly changing and as up-to-date and as automated as possible. In fact, there are many occasions when 'automation' can result in slower, less efficient operation; there are certainly many cases where existing equipment is perfectly adequate for the job and does not necessarily need to be replaced by the latest advanced models.

Of course, refusing to accept change and stubbornly sticking to old equipment that has long outlived its usefulness is just as damaging as the attitude that makes the office seem like an office automation showroom, with the latest equipment barely pausing as it passes through. Any new investment in office automation should produce a marked benefit, such as:

- More efficient use of time

- Reduced costs

- Better services to customers

- Faster results
- Greater availability of information
- More efficient storage and retrieval of information

You will never succeed in all of these and often there are trade-offs to be made.

Choosing office automation equipment

The computer alone provides a massive choice of systems for the first-time user. First there is the agonising choice over which model of computer; this is generally closely followed by decisions over which programs to run, what peripheral devices are needed (printers, plotters, etc.), whether standalone units or a network are required, and so on.

Putting your accounts on computer, for example, is only the start of it. This is only useful if you have a suitable printer to produce the necessary hard copy of the results: the invoices, statements and end-of-year accounts that must of

A Philips system in which up to eight workstations, each with its own dedicated processor, can be connected to undertake different tasks simultaneously

necessity be ultimately stored on paper. The paper-free office, so long promised yet now further away than ever, is an illusion we are unlikely to see reach fruition for many years to come. Indeed, most of those involved in any form of office automation will generally readily admit that the introduction of any new equipment usually results in an increase in paper.

It is important to get a very clear idea of why you want to invest in a particular piece of equipment. For many people the attraction of a new computer is that it is going to save them money. It should be realised from the very start that computers, or any other similar equipment for that matter, are unlikely to result in immediately obvious savings. There may be long-term financial benefits, but these are often hard to quantify.

The question of whether you will save time is also difficult to answer and depends greatly on the intended use of the machine. If the intention is to computerise the business accounts then certainly great savings in time may be derived, as long as you do not expect to get more from your accounts than you do at present.

The actual entry of accounts information is probably no faster than traditional manual methods. The savings come when the VAT accounts are due and your only task is to select the relevant option from the menu, wait for a few minutes and then transfer the final totals onto the VAT form.

However, for many people this is only the start. Why have all this information and power at your fingertips if you don't intend to make the maximum possible use of it? So the savings in time – and therefore the associated monetary savings – are soon swallowed up by the extra effort put into producing budgets, analyses of expenditure by department, detailed breakdowns of costs for individual projects and so on. The benefits have now been translated into improved efficiency and higher quality results. The trick is to ensure that these derived improvements lead to a more streamlined business, greater productivity or more customers.

The computer is therefore going to lead to a variety of benefits: savings in time, reduced costs, greater efficiency, more control, increased productivity or higher quality of work. You cannot have all of them; an increase in one is almost invariably matched by a decrease in another. The task of the office manager is to perform a delicate balancing act, expanding the automation only to areas where it is going to provide genuine enhancements to the overall situation.

Forward planning

Knowing precisely what the new equipment is going to be used for is the first

Plessey integrated switched digital exchange installed in an office

step in ensuring that the new wonder equipment does not end up as a white elephant.

You should have in mind a very clear overall strategy for the automation of your office. Each new acquisition should have been planned for at an early stage and preparations made so that when it actually arrives it fits comfortably into place without upsetting all the other elements of the office and without the need for a major reorganisation around it.

If you have a firm long-term plan then you can add and update new equipment as and when it is needed or can be afforded. The other alternative, to buy each item separately and without an overview of the whole system, results in irritating problems of incompatibility, wasted time and wasted resources.

The office automation environment

That is not to say that you should devise a rigid, inflexible plan and insist on sticking to it no matter what may happen. It is essential to be able to adapt to new circumstances. There will always be new equipment on the market, a device may not perform in the way you expect and your requirements may undergo radical changes as you adjust your working practices to new situations. Therefore you will need to have the strength of character to revise your plan as your office environment changes and the courage, if necessary, to throw out a redundant piece of equipment and start again.

It is at times like this that you should always remember that the system you buy should be flexible enough to fit in with your current working practices. If you have to change in order to accommodate the system then it is time to look very carefully to see if you really have the most suitable system for your needs. Before proceeding with any part of your office automation plan you should always have a very clear idea of what will be the savings and what are the costs; the knock-on effects on other areas of the organisation, whether good or bad, should also be clearly identified.

The hardest part is to be really objective and to control personal prejudices (whether they are in favour or against some new proposal). Keeping an open mind is not a virtue that is readily associated with automation. All too often bias against a particular technology delays its introduction or excessive enthusiasm results in the acquisition of unnecessary equipment. Don't be put off by the scare stories but, equally, don't be taken in by the glossy adverts.

Office automation targets

The first task, before you even open a magazine or glance at a brochure, is to decide exactly what problem it is you wish to solve. It is sometimes said that computers are solutions looking for a problem and this can be very close to the truth. Once any new machine has been installed it is remarkably easy to find new uses for it, but this is not generally a cost-effective way of proceeding.

Why do you need this particular type of machine? If it is because you think a business of your standing should have one, because someone has told you that you really should get one or because you think you can probably think of a use for it once it is installed then you should think again! A vast amount of money is spent on office automation equipment and far too high a proportion is wasted on systems that are not really needed or are never used.

If you are using comparisons with other offices to decide whether or not you ought to purchase more equipment then it is well worth looking around to see how much equipment they have lying around idle. An inspection of their stationery cupboards and beneath dust sheets can reveal a surprising level of surplus equipment, often in an 'as new' condition. The bulkiness of IBM PCs makes them unsuitable as paperweights, but in many offices they may just as well be that for all the good they do.

Hopefully you will go into the decision-making part of the deal with a very clear idea in your mind of what you want the machine to do. Not only does

With digital services becoming more widely available, this integrated services digital terminal from Philips allows simultaneous voice and data operation over a single pair of telephone wires

this save the purchase of unwanted equipment, it means you can build up the right sort of equipment from the very beginning. There is nothing more frustrating than buying a computer only to discover that the software you eventually decide you would like to run is not compatible with the hardware.

Learning from the mistakes of others is one of the best ways of avoiding the many potential pitfalls. Talking to others in a similar line of business is therefore a very good way of deciding whether a particular item is suited to your situation.

The potential uses can generally be divided into two categories: the essentials and the optional extras. While you should always bear in mind the other purposes for which the system may be used, in the long run this should not normally be the deciding factor. If the driving force is the computerisation of the stock control system, then an unsuitable system should not be purchased just because it has a rather nice graphics program attached.

When to buy

The greatest heart-searching comes in deciding when is actually the best time to buy. Studying the available literature relating to the branch of office automation in which you are interested soon shows you that the technology is changing very fast. New features are being added all the time and prices are generally falling. There is always some new product just around the corner.

However, if you always wait until the next predicted breakthrough you will never take the plunge. There is always a good time to buy, but there is also a danger of waiting too long. At the time of writing, for example, the cost of laser printers is still far too high for most small business to even consider, but the price is expected to drop dramatically over the next year or so. On the other hand, computer prices are now more stable than they have ever been and this is as good a time to buy as any. It is true that in twelve months' time there will undoubtedly have been major advances, but anything you buy now will represent a respectable long-term investment.

The comparisons you make should not be between the machines that are available now and some imaginary future developments, but between your business as it now operates and what it would be like with the introduction of the new equipment. This will usually show you that the improvements you can make in the coming months from the machines you purchase now will easily offset any savings that may be made by waiting for the next generation of equipment to come along.

The agonising does not necessarily end with the decision to buy. If you are to retain your peace of mind once the deed has been done there are a few important rules to set yourself:

- Steel yourself for the fact that the week after you have made your purchase a new model will be announced that has far superior features, is faster, has more memory, and is cheaper than your own machine. If you do find this infuriating then you can comfort yourself with the knowledge that the person who buys this new machine will no doubt soon find himself in the same situation!

- Be satisfied with what you have and don't waste time poring over the latest advertisements. There may be something better around the corner, but the machine you have bought still represents incredible value for money. Remember that even five years ago the facilities you now have at your fingertips would probably have seemed like an idle dream.

- Accept that the machine is going to depreciate rapidly, probably even faster than your accountant writes it off. Even if you keep it in perfect order it is unlikely that anyone will want to buy such an outdated machine second-hand, even in only three or four years' time.

- Bear in mind that the expense has only just begun. Your new acquisition will need to be kept supplied with all sorts of 'consumables' – ribbons, paper, disks, etc.

Compatibility

The way in which the various components of an office automation system fit together is a crucial factor in determining whether or not the system is a success.

First of all there is the compatibility of the computer systems. Check that the chosen system can communicate with any other computers you may have or may need to deal with. For example, if you need to transfer data from one machine to another using a floppy disk, make sure that the disks produced by one machine can actually be read by the other; it is not sufficient to know that they are the same size and that they look the same.

Next you need to be sure that the programs you want to run are actually available in versions that the computer can use. This is where the greatest difficulty lies. Having decided that the Apple Macintosh is what is really needed because of its desktop publishing capabilities, it is no good settling for Sage Accounts, which runs on IBM-compatibles. More of this discussion continues in the chapters on computers and software, but the basic rule for buying any form of equipment is to see the component parts demonstrated working together before you buy.

This principle applies equally to all parts of the system. Printers, for example, are very pedantic about how they can be connected to computers and programs; laser printers in particular should always be tested in full with your chosen software.

This discussion is not meant to be offputting; really it comes down to a little caution and common sense. After all, if you want new parts for a Renault you would not go to a Ford dealer.

The simplest rule is to assume that no two products are going to be able to work smoothly together unless you actually see them being operated satisfactorily.

It is worth noting that compatibility is slowly but surely becoming a problem of the past. Not only are different makes of computer becoming more compatible as more manufacturers adopt the IBM standard, but other categories of office automation product are also beginning to adopt set standards. Facsimile machines, for example, conform to quite rigidly defined standards that ensure that any two machines in the same class can communicate.

Convergence

As well as this improvement in compatibility within categories of machine, we are now seeing all the various groups moving closer together and it is becoming more and more common for links to be made between totally different machines, as they all begin to speak the same language. In the middle of all this is the telephone network which is now a major link for all forms of communication device.

This process is called *convergence*. The digital language of the computer is now being adopted by most branches of the office automation world.

Computers are really very simple devices, when you get down to the basics. The 'language' that they can understand is called *binary* and consists of only two characters, 0 and 1. Physically these are represented by the presence or absence of an electric pulse or by the polarity of a magnetic field.

All of the computer's programs and its entire operation is based upon machine code that is built entirely from these characters. Any instruction or piece of data can be constructed from a string of binary digits, or *bits*, in much the same way that Morse code is constructed from strings of dots and dashes (but much more systematically). A string of eight bits is known as a *byte*.

There are 256 possible combinations of zeros and ones in a byte so each byte is generally used to represent a single character of data. The first 128 combinations provide sufficient codes to represent all upper and lower case letters, the numbers 0 to 9 and an extensive list of punctuation marks, arithmetical symbols and other characters. There is a standard table for converting these characters, which are called *ASCII* codes. (ASCII stands for American Standard Code for Information Interchange.)

The other 128 combinations are generally used for graphics characters, foreign letters, mathematical symbols and so on, but the standardisation here is not so secure.

By converting data in any internal format to ASCII format any program is therefore usually able to convert its data to a form that can be understood by another program. Similarly data in ASCII format can be transferred to any other make of computer provided each machine has a suitable program for transmitting and receiving such data. This format is also used for passing data to a printer.

This *digital* coding of information is now being adopted by the telephone network, as the old analogue equipment is phased out. The advantage of digital information is that you can build in various checks to ensure that no mistakes have occurred during the transmission and, if they have, they can be corrected. By contrast, the infinitely variable analogue signals of the old networks were very open to interference and distortion.

Digital data from a computer can thus pass down a digital telephone line to be picked up at the other end by any other piece of digital equipment. The latest standards for facsimile machines are based upon digital methods so there is now no reason why information should not be transferred from computer to facsimile and back again.

It is not only text and numbers that can be converted to digital format. Pictures and graphic images can be represented in digital form. Any image on the computer screen is made up from thousands – in some cases, millions – of individual coloured dots, called *pixels* (an abbreviation for 'picture elements'). Pictures from television cameras are converted to the same form, but with a much higher intensity of dots.

Sound, too, is succumbing to the fashion for conversion to digital format, and not just in the telephone world. The arrival of compact discs proves not only that sound can be converted into this simple form, but that the quality is actually enhanced in the process. In addition this data can be stored in a permanent form, to be 'read' by lasers, so that the quality never diminishes.

Thus there is a convergence of all sorts of apparently distinct technologies, with there being no reason why any form of information should not ultimately be passed freely amongst them all.

However, there is still a long way to go. We may have perfected the art of converting the human voice into a digital form for transfer along the telephone networks, but programming a computer to decipher this data into something meaningful is still not even remotely feasible on any widespread scale. There are machines that can understand quite large vocabularies of carefully spoken words; the computer with which you can hold an intelligent conversation is still something for the future.

Chapter 2

Buying office automation equipment

Buying any new equipment can be a harassing experience so it should be taken slowly and in several stages. Decide roughly what you need, get a demonstration, think it over and discuss it with colleagues – and then make sure that help will be on hand to sort out problems afterwards.

The first stage is to decide exactly what you want to achieve. Write it down and don't be pressurised into adding features you don't really need. Get a general idea of what the alternatives are and what facilities you can expect to get for the budget that is available. Armed with this information, head for a reputable dealer, preferably one that has been recommended to you from a trustworthy source. The dealer should be able to help point you in the right direction, but don't be forced along any route you do not want to take.

Making the most of demonstrations

Never be afraid to ask the dealer or salesman for a full demonstration of the product, especially if it is at the expensive end of the price range. In particular, make sure that it will work with any existing equipment you have. If possible you should insist on sitting down with the machine or software yourself for a little while to make sure it really does what you want it to and that it is as easy to operate as they say.

The danger is that if you are unfamiliar with a technology you may not be aware of the pitfalls and the restrictions of individual products. It is very easy to attach to a product powers that simply do not exist.

The main problem with any pre-planned demonstration is that it is often performed at such a speed that it is impossible to take in all the new information you are seeing. This is not necessarily because the salesman is trying to fool you into believing the product can achieve more than it can. It is simply a fact that once anyone becomes familiar with a system its use can – and should – become second nature. (Indeed, if six months after purchase you still have to refer to the manual to carry out common tasks then the user-friendliness of the system is obviously suspect!)

Also, any complex sequence of key strokes or rapid succession of screen displays presents so much information in a short space of time that it is impossible to digest it all. After all, the person selling the product is engaged in the legitimate task of trying to prove to you that with a little experience the result can be achieved quickly and effectively so he or she will not want to work painstakingly through from one part of the sequence to the next.

The equipment should be fully tested. For example, if you have any fears that the chosen facsimile machine may not be able to communicate with the machine at head office or that of your major contractor, then arrange for a sample message to be sent. This has a number of benefits. Firstly you can satisfy yourself that the device will actually do what you set out to achieve (and it should also satisfy the dealer that you are not going to be coming back in a few days time to get him to sort out communications problems).

It will also give you a good idea of how long it really takes to carry out the operation and how easy it is. The person giving the demonstration will inevitably be extremely slick at following through the standard demonstration procedures. He or she should also be an experienced operator of the equipment. Therefore the difficulties they encounter in trying to perform some task that you have specified will give a good indication of how long it will really take you, once you become familiar with the system. It will also show how fast the equipment performs when asked to do something other than the previously prepared demo.

A non-standard demonstration is bound to take a little longer, for the reasons already given, but any really significant difference in operation should prompt you to ask why it cannot be carried out so smoothly. Even if you are given a satisfactory answer you should insist on further experiments to satisfy yourself that the system does not only work with one set of data!

If the demonstrator indicates that they are unable to carry out the test you require because they are not sufficiently *au fait* with the equipment then ask for someone who is. If the answer is 'Sorry, they're not available at the moment' then this should be an indication to you that maybe you should look elsewhere; at the very least you should make an appointment for a time when someone is available. When you have made your purchase you will almost

Tandon Target demonstrating the EGA option

certainly need a little specialist advice to get you going. You want to be sure that it is going to be there when you need it.

Of course, this does not mean that the sales team can be expected to be walking encyclopaedias, with the answer to every question at their fingertips. They should be familiar with the basics and they should at least know where to look for the answers to any tricky problems you may come up with. An offer to find out the answer is just as good as the answer itself, as long as it is followed up fairly quickly and results in a satisfactory response.

This initial decision period is a testing time for both the dealer and the buyer. Although you are checking the competence of the dealer as well as the performance of the machine, this does not mean that you should set unfair and unreasonable tests. Just because no-one can tell you what chip is at the heart of the fax or what language the spreadsheet is written in, does not imply that they will not have the answer when the machine fails to operate correctly. Asking out of genuine interest is one thing, pure awkwardness is quite another. If the question is unimportant then the lack of an answer is also of little consequence.

This is your chance to make sure that the complete package (including after-sales service) is satisfactory and also that this really is what you are after. Never be afraid to change your mind if you realise that the product is not quite so amazing as you originally thought. You will not lose face by changing direction and looking elsewhere before money changes hands; you will feel very foolish if you end up with a product that fails the major tests your colleagues set.

Don't be put off asking for a full demonstration, either by the sales staff's apparent unwillingness to show you the equipment or your own desire not to be a nuisance. If they seem in a hurry, it's nearly lunch time or whatever other problem may lie in the way, then you should make arrangements for a demonstration another time. After all, if they are not prepared to go out of their way to help when they are on the verge of making a profit from you, what use are they going to be when you go back to them with problems later?

It is only rarely that you will come across problems of the type described above, but it is as well to know that there are a very few unreliable dealers about. Most dealers in office automation equipment are extremely trustworthy and helpful at all stages, from the first tentative enquiries right through to the final sale and after-sales service.

Just as with buying a new car, a test drive is always a good idea. The salesman may show you how easily the word processor can mark and delete a block of text, but having to explain to you how it is done may well reveal the sleight-of-hand for what it really is. The eye does not see the deft movement of the hand over the keyboard as the demonstrator performs this particular piece of magic. When you try to repeat the trick yourself you may find that is is not that simple after all, as you discover that the beginning of the block is marked by pressing the Control key in combination with K and B, the end with Control-KK and the disappearing act is completed by the magic words Control-KY. Obvious, isn't it?! (In actual fact this obscure operation is part of the 'industry standard' word-processing program, WordStar; more of that in Chapter 6.)

This brings us to the subject of documentation.

User-friendliness, help screens and documentation

The fact that the main commands used by a program are not ones that trip easily off the tongue, is not necessarily an indication that the program is hard to use or that it lacks *user-friendliness*. This ghastly term refers to how simple a program appears to the person who uses it.

Fortunately, the days are now passing when unscrupulous salesmen tried to confuse us with a stream of jargon and the writers of manuals and magazine articles sought to impress the uninitiated by computerised name-dropping, littering their text with such terms as contention-based access protocols, bus topology and proprietary blocked-asynchronous transmission (from an article on choosing local area networks). 'User-friendliness' is the buzzword of the moment, so everyone is trying to make their products seem as natural as possible; this has to be a major step forward.

Unfortunately this does mean that some of the products end up with documentation that takes friendliness to nauseating extremes. 'User-chumminess' may be a better term in these cases.

You can easily test the user-friendliness of your proposed package by pressing a few wrong keys. For example, if asked to press either Y or N (for 'Yes' or 'No'), try pressing a totally different key. At the very least the program should beep at you and in some cases you should expect a warning message to be given. Next try entering a lower-case Y. Few modern programs don't take the trouble to convert your entry to capitals, but there are still some around.

```
Y                          WordStar Professional Release 4

Specify the document that you wish to be permanently erased from disk.
If you do not specify a drive in the document name, it will be erased
from drive C.

You can stop any erasure from occurring by typing ^U (press the U
key while holding down the CTRL control key).

Document to be erased? *.bak
 ↵ done    | Backspace or ^H erase left | ^X move cursor to directory
  ^U cancel |              Del erase      |
Are you sure (Y/N)? R
Please press Y for yes, or N for no.
DIRECTORY   Drive C:\MORRIS  2.6M free
 .4k OAFGCAPS        .3k OAFGCAPS.BAK   2.1k OAPREF          13k OAPRELS
```

The user-friendliness of WordStar4

When a value outside an allowed range is entered, the program should reject the value and ask you to re-enter. If the range is not an obvious one, you should be told what values are acceptable. In particular, dates can cause problems if not properly handled by the program. When the program asks for a date, try entering 29/02/88 and 29/02/87. The first should be accepted, the second rejected.

With a good product, whether hardware or software, you should be able to sit down and get it working without any further training or extensive reference to the manual. Of course, this is not a particularly good idea, especially if you

```
JI                        WordStar Professional Release 4
                          O P E N I N G   M E N U
    D open a document                    L change logged drive/directory
    N open a nondocument                 C protect a file
    P print a file                       E rename a file
    M merge print a file                 O copy a file
    I index a document                   Y delete a file
    T table of contents                  F turn directory off
    X exit WordStar                    Esc shorthand
    J help                               R run a DOS command

I (index a document) creates an index for a document you name.  You can
index every word in your document, or just the ones following the .IX dot
command or surrounded by ^K's.  Your index file will have the same name as
your document, with the special extension .IDX.

See the Reference Guide in your manual for more information.

Press Esc to continue.
```

Help screen from WordStar4

are a novice. Most good programs are pretty idiot-proof but, at least until you have made copies of the original disks, you should avoid the temptation to start pressing keys to see what happens. Most suppliers are very good about reconstructing a wrecked original disk, but it's better not to push your luck!

Many programs now incorporate on-screen help displays. By pressing a special key (function key F1 is the one most commonly used on the IBM range) your work screen is replaced by a screenful of helpful information relevant to the particular operation you are carrying out. After reading it you can return to your original place in the program. That's the theory; in practice it may not work quite so smoothly so it is worth checking on the facility if one is provided. But remember that with a good program you should soon master all but the most complex operations and the help displays should not then be of great importance.

An inspection of the manual is just as important a part of your preliminary enquiries. You will certainly need to refer to the manual to find out how to set up the program in the first instance and to investigate some of its more interesting but less obvious features. There are often little tricks described in the manual for overcoming certain problems or for making the program easier to work with that you can never get by trial and error.

The program should be learnt in easy stages. You will certainly not be able to take in all the information in the manual the first time you read it. Once the basics have been mastered you can go on to investigate its more interesting properties. The more advanced features of a program should only be attempted when you are fully in control of the basic program.

Therefore you need a manual that is simple to use, clearly and concisely written and is adequately equipped with either a good reference section or a comprehensive index – or both. Any special features of the program should be kept firmly in perspective (unlike one famous case in which the first few chapters of a word-processor manual proudly described the ways in which all the words in a document could be rearranged in alphabetical order, with the description of how to save a document on disk being relegated to an appendix!).

If the manual is confusing or less than complete then it is not the end of the world; if the program or equipment is good enough you can get by. It does mean, though, that you will have to invest in a good book on the product, make numerous phone calls to your dealer or other users or attend training.

The cooling-off period

When the criteria you have set have all been met and the final decision to purchase has been taken, it is as well to wait a little longer before concluding the deal. There is no statutory 'cooling-off period' as there is with life insurance, but nevertheless, unless you are desperate for the new equipment, it is a good idea to wait a day or two. This gives you time to think about what you have chosen, to have a final chat with those who are going to use it and to ensure that you have not been persuaded to buy something you don't really want.

This is also a good time to ask the dealer for the names of others like yourself who have bought a similar system. A brief discussion with an established user will help you get a feel for the system and what it can achieve in the real world. It should also result in some helpful tips and give you an idea of any shortcomings of the product and how these may be avoided. Remember that the dealer is unlikely to point you in the direction of anyone who has expressed dissatisfaction with the system.

After-sales service

Your relationship with the dealer should not end when you walk out of his door with your brand new product. By that time you should have a very good idea of how he/she will respond when you go back later for help and advice. Most dealers regard a limited amount of free verbal assistance as a part of the deal and will gladly help out.

Whatever you buy should have at least a twelve months' guarantee and, of course, there are all the usual statutory rights to protect you. In some cases you will be offered an extended guarantee period for an additional fee. Whether or not you take this up depends very much upon the equipment you have bought. It becomes a question of balancing up the costs on both sides. In many cases, for example when buying computers, the equipment will be robust enough for you to take the risk that the machine will not stay the course.

After a few years you will almost certainly want to replace the computer with something more advanced – and probably cheaper – and by that time the computer will have lost most of its value anyway.

For other equipment and for the more expensive computer systems and networks some form of maintenance agreement is probably a good idea. When buying a photocopier, however, which is basically a mechanical device with a lot of delicate components to go wrong, then an extended period is almost certainly well worth the extra investment. These topics are covered in greater depth in chapter 11.

Chapter 3

Computers in the office

Computers are at the heart of the office automation revolution. The microprocessor chips on which they are based also form the core of most of the other equipment that is operated in the office. Facsimile machines, photocopiers, printers and 'intelligent' telephones all derive their powers from the tiny computer chips at the centre of their circuits.

All these other devices are dedicated to performing one particular set of tasks: transmitting printed information, duplicating text and diagrams or sending voice communications around the world. Computers, on the other hand, provide a flexible base upon which you can build any number of different applications. With the right additions you can write a report, plan a budget, send an invoice, create a job estimate or produce charts for use on overhead projectors. There will also be applications specifically related to your type of business, from monitoring water levels to labelling medicine bottles.

This chapter looks at computers, what you need, the separate components and their capabilities, and introduces the programs that temporarily convert your blank computer into a dedicated machine.

Computer systems

The computer industry has come a long way in the last few years. The arrival of the microchip has meant that computing power that was previously only available on large and inaccessible mainframes can now be present on a corner of the desk at a cost that is no more than the price of a few hour's access to its mainframe predecessor.

It is no longer the case that you have to wear a white coat in order to even approach the computer room; anyone can become a computer 'expert', mastering one or more fields of the technology and treating it as second nature. The mystique of the Fifties and Sixties that elevated computer operators to the level of high priests has now been largely dissipated. There are still those who try to maintain the exclusivity of the computer world by enshrouding their activities in the jargon that is the mumbo-jumbo of the computer religion. In the main however, there is little reason why anyone who is unfamiliar with the technology should not become adept at using it in a very short time.

It is hard to believe that only ten or twelve years ago the most advanced commercial computers came in kit form and had to be assembled on the kitchen table before they could perform any useful task. Even then many of them struggled to remember a single page of A4 text. To-day's descendents of those early home computers arrive ready to be plugged in, at roughly the same cost, with memories that can store the equivalent of the average novel.

Computer compatibility

Gone are the days when every model of computer had its own totally individual way of operating, making it a hopeless proposition to transfer information and programs between different models. The introduction of the IBM PC in 1982 may have turned the computer world upside down and inflicted an inferior machine on millions of people, but it also did a great service in ensuring that compatibility between machines would become a major driving force in the design of new computers.

Up until that point each manufacturer was trying to cut himself as large a slice of the computer cake as possible. Being individual had a number of advantages. Firstly the manufacturer could claim to be making significant breakthroughs and offer functions that were not present on their rivals' machines.

Secondly, once they had attracted a customer, that person was stuck to their products when it became time to upgrade, unless they wanted to undertake the expensive tasks of re-entering data onto the new machine and buying a completely new selection of programs.

For both user and manufacturer there were very great disadvantages in the gamble being undertaken. If the machine did not prove popular then few software companies were prepared to write programs for it; the lack of software discouraged other potential users from buying the machine and this vicious circle hastened the end of many small computer companies. A few took off and went from strength to strength; the majority fell by the wayside and perished quickly. There must still be thousands of redundant computers cluttering up store cupboards around the world, a painful reminder of the waste of money attached to choosing the wrong system.

The IBM success story

Fortunately it is now much harder to make the wrong choice. The introduction of the IBM PC proved to be a turning point from which there was no turning back. IBM were assured of success even before they entered the market. An established company – one of the largest in the world – with a proven track record and a reputation for reliability, they could not go wrong.

Everyone knew that IBM mainframes had been around for decades and that the company was well and truly here to stay. This was the complete opposite of the experiences associated with most of the smaller companies that had rapidly soared to fame, only to spectacularly crash soon afterwards, leaving disgruntled customers amongst the ruins wondering what they were going to do with the expensive hardware that had become unfashionable and unserviceable overnight.

The IBM Personal Computer

IBM PC AT

It did not seem to matter that the first IBM PC was noisy, expensive, slow and not particularly attractive. The IBM label guaranteed that the predicted success was a self-fulfilling prophecy. Everyone said that the machine was sure to be a success, so everyone bought the machine and made it a success.

Just as the vicious circle of software was the death knell of many unknown hardware companies, so the escalating success of the IBM resulted in an upward spiral of new software and new customers that made it invincible. Needless to say, IBM products still top the bestseller lists.

Enforced compatibility

With the customers rapidly converging on IBM it became essential for manufacturers to conform to the standards set by the new computer.

The latest IBM PC – the Personal System/2

Compatibility with IBM gave them access to all the software being written for the PC and also meant that customers could be sure that no matter what happened they would be able to transfer to a similar machine, or any new versions that came along, without losing their data or programs.

That, at any rate, was the theory. As it turned out the term 'compatibility' was very loosely interpreted in many cases and frequently a machine that was termed 'compatible' turned out to be very selective in which parts of it were interchangeable with IBM PCs.

Many new compatible machines were launched. Some of them have been lasting successes (Olivetti, for example), while others have struggled to gain acceptance. In particular there have been many new imported IBM 'clones', machines that claim to resemble the PC in all levels of operation. In most cases these prove to be a very satisfactory substitute for the IBM PC and at a greatly reduced price.

Most successful companies now include an IBM-compatible in their range; the majority are now exclusively dealing in compatible computers. The British company, Apricot (formerly ACT), are a prime example of a

Apricot XEN computers

company with a good idea of its own that was forced to move to IBM-compatibility, but only just in time. At the same time that the original IBM PC was being marketed the first Apricot PC was being sold in very large numbers. It proved a very successful machine and is still widely used, though now no longer available in the shops.

The Apricot PC scored over IBM in many ways: a crisper, higher resolution screen display, 3½-inch disks that were more robust than IBM's 5¼-inch and capable of storing much more information, faster, more compact and reasonably portable. It lacked just one important thing – compatibility. Even so, the Apricot PC will be fondly remembered by most people in much the same way as they recall their first car.

These early machines brought great success to Apricot and established a large user-base. This prompted the company to launch an exotic range of 'F' machines; sadly these failed to make an impact on the market. Compatibility was beginning to become a keyword and the range proved almost disastrous for the company. Apricot retrenched and the machines disappeared after a very short time, to be replaced by the fast and powerful XEN. This machine has now been joined by the XEN-i, an IBM-compatible that will surely keep Apricot at the forefront of the computer industry in Britain for several years to come.

A similar tale can be told of the Apple computers. The Apple II was a tremendously successful American computer that gained very wide acceptance and huge success. It came in a number of forms. This was followed by the Macintosh, which introduced the concepts of windows, icons and mouse to many people for the first time (more on these later). However, for many years Apple insisted on following their own very different path, a route that could not go on for ever. After all, if it were to become a match between IBM

Apple Macintosh

and Apple, then there really could be no contest. So it is that the latest Macintosh's now boast IBM-compatibility.

Other IBM-compatibles

Not all computers are named after varieties of fruit! (Legend has it that the Apple was so named because, while struggling to find a name, one of the founders was eating an apple and declared that unless they thought of something else by five o'clock then Apple would be the name; presumably they were short on inspiration that day.)

The IBM-compatible that has created the most publicity in recent years is the Amstrad PC. In a similar way to the IBM, these new machines were almost assured of success before they were launched because everyone believed that success was a certainty. Of course, they have some very important factors in their favour.

Firstly they are very cheap; this makes them affordable by many small businesses who could not have considered such an investment in the past. The Amstrad PC forms a bridge between the business market and the home enthusiasts. Secondly, the company is well respected and reliable, not only because of its earlier computers but also because of its success in other fields. Thirdly, the computer is genuinely IBM-compatible. There are very few applications that cause problems on the Amstrad and most Amstrad programs operate very successfully on the IBM PC.

Amstrad PC1640

Another major advantage is that the Amstrad PC also *looks* like a professional computer. Any office manager can be reasonably satisfied with an Amstrad on his desk; what self-respecting businessman could look professional with a Sinclair QL doing its impersonation of a novelty cigar box? Looks may not be important in real terms, but a professional image is important. Indeed there are many people who prefer to pay for the higher-priced clones because they do not feel that such a cheap machine can give them the right image. In fact the Amstrad PC is fast gaining respectability by being bought in large quantities by businesses of all sizes, local authorities and many other organisations.

The Amstrad PC1512, launched in the autumn of 1986, was followed in 1987 by the PC1640, a computer with 25% more memory and a high-resolution colour display.

Other compatibles are marketed by Olivetti (a very successful range), Sanyo, Ferranti and Xenith. These are all sound investments and each has something of its own to offer.

However, now that everyone else has learnt to play the game it looks as if IBM are all set to change the rules.

Amstrad PCW9512 word processor

Also worth considering is the Amstrad PCW9512, commonly known as the Amstrad Word Processor. This machine is equipped with its own printer and an excellent word-processing program. This machine is certainly worth looking at if dealing with text is your most important task. Although marketed for its word-processing capabilities the PCW is in fact a fully fledged computer, capable of running a range of other programs, such as databases and accounts packages. The PCW is not IBM-compatible so the range of software is inevitably limited. It also uses non-standard 3-inch disks, which can make the servicing of the machine expensive.

Choosing a computer

There are a number of considerations to be made when choosing a computer:

Price The variations in price are not as great as they have been in the past but even so you can expect to make quite considerable savings by shopping around from one manufacturer to another, and one dealer to another. Even machines that offer the same or similar facilities can vary in price quite considerably. There is no point paying extra for features that you just do not need.

Range of software It helps to have a wide range of software available but that is not essential. The important thing is to ensure that you will have access to the programs you need.

Memory To store programs and data, computers need memory, the more the better. If you choose anything less than 512K you will be limited in the programs you can run. (See below for further details.)

Screen displays You can generally choose between monochrome and colour displays, but in addition there is a wide variation in the clarity of the displays. The display type has a great impact on price, so careful consideration needs to be given here. Of course it is pleasant to have a high resolution, colour displayS but is it really necessary if the main task for the machine is to be stock control?

Disk drives How you are going to store data is an important consideration and will depend upon how much information you need to store and how accessible that information needs to be.

Speed Different computers operate at different speeds. To the new owner they probably all seem remarkably fast. It is only when you run the same program on two different machines that the difference in operating speed becomes apparent. To give an idea of the variations between models, the Amstrad PC is about four times as fast as the IBM PC. This does not mean that it will take you four times as long to perform the same operation on the IBM PC; most of the time the speed depends on how quickly you respond, since most applications rely heavily upon operator input. It is when a program has to draw a complicated screen display or perform some long and complex calculations that the differences may become apparent.

Therefore, whether you need this extra speed largely depends upon the applications to be run. For word processing, accounts and stock control, and any other applications where the speed is heavily dependant upon how quickly the operator can enter information, the speed of the microprocessor is not of great importance. Speed does become a major factor when buying a system to perform substantial data-handling, for example to condense large volumes of data into smaller files or to draw complex graphs based on large stores of raw data. In such circumstances the addition of a maths co-processor may be an advantage (see Chapter 5).

Compatibility As described above, sitting computers next to each other does not necessarily mean that they will be able to talk to each other. IBM-compatibility is, of course, one consideration, but it is not the only one. Do you need to pass data to another computer or exchange programs? If so then you need to find out exactly what equipment you need to be compatible with; this will include not only the computer itself but its display type, whether it is fitted with any additional chips or cards and so on.

If you are not concerned about communicating with other computers or preparing data in a format suitable for other computers then your only concern need be for your own future requirements when you come to move on to the next generation of computers. If, at some time in the future, you may want to transfer data and programs to a new system, IBM-compatibility should be considered; if your chosen machine does not conform you will need assurances from your dealer that the company will be around in a few years time, that it will be manufacturing more advanced machines and that any new products from the manufacturer will be compatible with their earlier machines.

It is normal for manufacturers to build in *upwards-compatibility*, i.e. each new machine can handle most of the programs and data from its predecessor. The reverse is not generally true. For example the disks from the early IBM PCs can be read quite happily by the newer models but special techniques need to be adopted to make data flow easily in the opposite direction.

If none of these considerations seems important then you are free to plump for the computer that offers the software you need.

Components of computers

When buying a computer there are a number of decisions to be made, apart from choosing the model itself. Most computers are sold in a variety of *configurations*, i.e. assortments of basic components. The parts of the computer system that may vary include:

- *Memory* The amount of information that can be held internally by the machine determines the efficiency and speed with which it is able to handle data; too little memory limits the programs that can be run.
- *Disk drives* The method used for permanent storage of programs and data has a major impact on price.
- *Monitor* The type of screen you choose determines the clarity of the display. Some programs have minimum display requirements that must be met for the program to run satisfactorily.

The above components are termed the computer *hardware*. Each of these components is described in more detail below. In addition there is a range of peripheral equipment from which to select. These extra items are described in Chapter 4.

Memory

To carry out its chosen task the computer needs a *program*, i.e. a list of instructions. The instructions usually result in the creation of information, which when stored in a computer is generally termed *data*; the two terms are generally regarded as being synonymous. These instructions, along with some of the data, have to be stored inside the computer in its *memory*.

Like the human memory, this is an internal area where information of any type can be stored. The memory is physically stored on a set of chips with vast arrays of cells, each of which can independently store instructions or values.

Just like the human memory, the memory of the computer is limited. There is a maximum capacity for the amount of information the computer can store at any one time. The computer generally has two types of memory:

- *Read Only Memory (ROM)* This is a part of memory that is set when you get the machine and cannot be changed. It is here that the programs needed to get the machine up and running are stored.

- *Random Access Memory (RAM)* This is the part of memory you are really interested in. Most of this memory can be used to store your programs, and is used by the programs to store data. The more memory the machine has, the larger the programs it can hold.

When purchasing a computer you may be told about other types of memory. For example, some computers have a small amount of battery-backed RAM, which is used for storing – and updating – information such as the current date and time when the mains power is switched off. This is extremely useful but not essential. Other terms may be applied to the type of memory but basically what you need to know is whether it can satisfactorily store the programs you want to run.

The size of memory is measured in *kilobytes*. Remembering that one byte can hold one character (for most purposes), a kilobyte can hold approximately 1000 bytes. (For the purist, it is actually 1024, which is 2 to the power 10.) One kilobyte is generally abbreviated to 1K. If you want to talk in terms of really large memories then the term *megabyte* is used, one megabyte (or 1M) being the equivalent of 1000K.

To put this into context, an average A4 sheet of text would use about 2.5K of memory.

The size of computer memories has grown dramatically over the last few years as the cost of producing the chips has come down and the designers have developed new systems of addressing vast units of memory.

The first IBM PC was equipped with 64K of RAM. Few programs these days could satisfactorily work with such a limited memory and the minimum you will expect to find in a business computer is 256K. For many applications this is still too small, with either the programs failing with 'Out of memory' messages or being considerably slowed up because they have to keep reading new parts of the program into memory and temporarily store data away.

For this reason the smallest memory available on machines such as the Amstrad PC1512 is 512K. This is enough for most needs but can be expanded if necessary by fitting additional memory chips. The successor to this machine, the PC1640 has a memory of 640K. The operating system on which all programs are based is, in many cases, limited to this amount of memory.

Don't be persuaded to buy machines with larger memory than this unless you are absolutely certain that the programs really need more and that they can actually use the extra memory.

Disk drives

There is another drawback to computer memory, apart from its limited size; the RAM upon which most applications are based needs a constant power supply to maintain its contents. Any interruption in the power supply, even if it is only momentary, results in the memory being irrevocably wiped clean.

This happens when you switch the computer off, when someone pulls out the wrong plug, when there is a temporary loss of power (such as in a thunder storm) and sometimes when there is a sudden surge in power. However, it should not cause a problem.

Just as people can only store a limited amount of information and need to refer to books to read in new information or refresh their memories on some subject they have forgotten, so computers need an external means of storing data and programs.

The method adopted by most modern microcomputers is that of *disks*. These are circular and coated in a magnetic material that can store computer data. In much the same way that a cassette tape can record and replay sound or be wiped clean, so the computer can store data on the surface of a disk, read it back into memory or wipe everything from the surface. In most cases any redundant data that has been written on disks can be overwritten with new information or updated.

The type of disk you use depends upon the the type of drive fitted in your machine. The majority of machines rely upon two basic types of disk:

- *Floppy disks* These are cheap, flexible disks that can generally store between 100K and 1000K of data. To be precise they should be called 'diskettes' but this term is rarely used, save in manuals. Floppy disks are interchangeable, i.e. you can take one disk out of the drive and replace it with another, so the amount of data available to your computer is limited only by the number of disks you buy.

- *Hard disks* Also known as 'fixed disks' and 'Winchesters', these disks can store much greater volumes of data than their floppy counterparts. Their capacities are measured in megabytes, typical sizes being 10M and 20M. Much larger disks are available, either built into the computer or as separate units. The advantages of hard disks include their capacity (a 10M hard disk stores the equivalent of 29 IBM floppies) and much faster access times.

Floppy disks come in various shapes and sizes. Very little is seen these days of the old-style 8½-inch disks, but you will come across the following:

- *5¼-inch* The most common type, needing careful handling to avoid damage. Sometimes called 'minidisks'.

- *3½-inch* These much more robust disks were pioneered by Apricot whose PC was the first to use them in volume. Not only are they smaller but they can hold more information than other types of disk. They are often referred to as 'microfloppies'.

- *3-inch* A very few machines use 3-inch disks, most notably the Amstrad PCW8256 and PCW8512. They tend to be rather more expensive than other types of floppy disk and are unlikely to become popular, despite being reliable and encased in a rigid plastic case.

There have also been other experiments with storage media, such as the microcassette tapes that were used – not very successfully – in the Sinclair QL and the ICL One-Per-Desk/Merlin Tonto.

Most manufacturers offer a choice between various combinations:

- *Single floppy drive* The cheapest option and not particularly satisfactory. Many programs need constant access to both a program disk and a data disk; copying a floppy disk is extremely tiresome if you have only one drive. Very few single-drive machines are sold these days. They can be useful if the machine is to be used mainly as a terminal linked to a mainframe.

- *Double floppy drive* With two drives most problems are overcome, unless you have very large programs that spill over onto more than a single floppy. In most cases, double-drive machines are the most commonly sold.

- *Hard disk (with a floppy drive as well)* These are the most expensive versions but provide the opportunity to store large quantities of programs and data without having to use irritating floppies.

Whatever configuration you buy you should be able to update it later if you find it is insufficient for your needs.

Monitors

The range of monitors available is perhaps most perplexing of all. Generally you have a choice between two alternatives:

- *Monochrome* These are the 'black and white' sets of the computer world. Text and graphics are displayed in one colour only, on a single-colour background. Originally the most common variety were the 'green'

Samsung MP5671 paper-white monitor

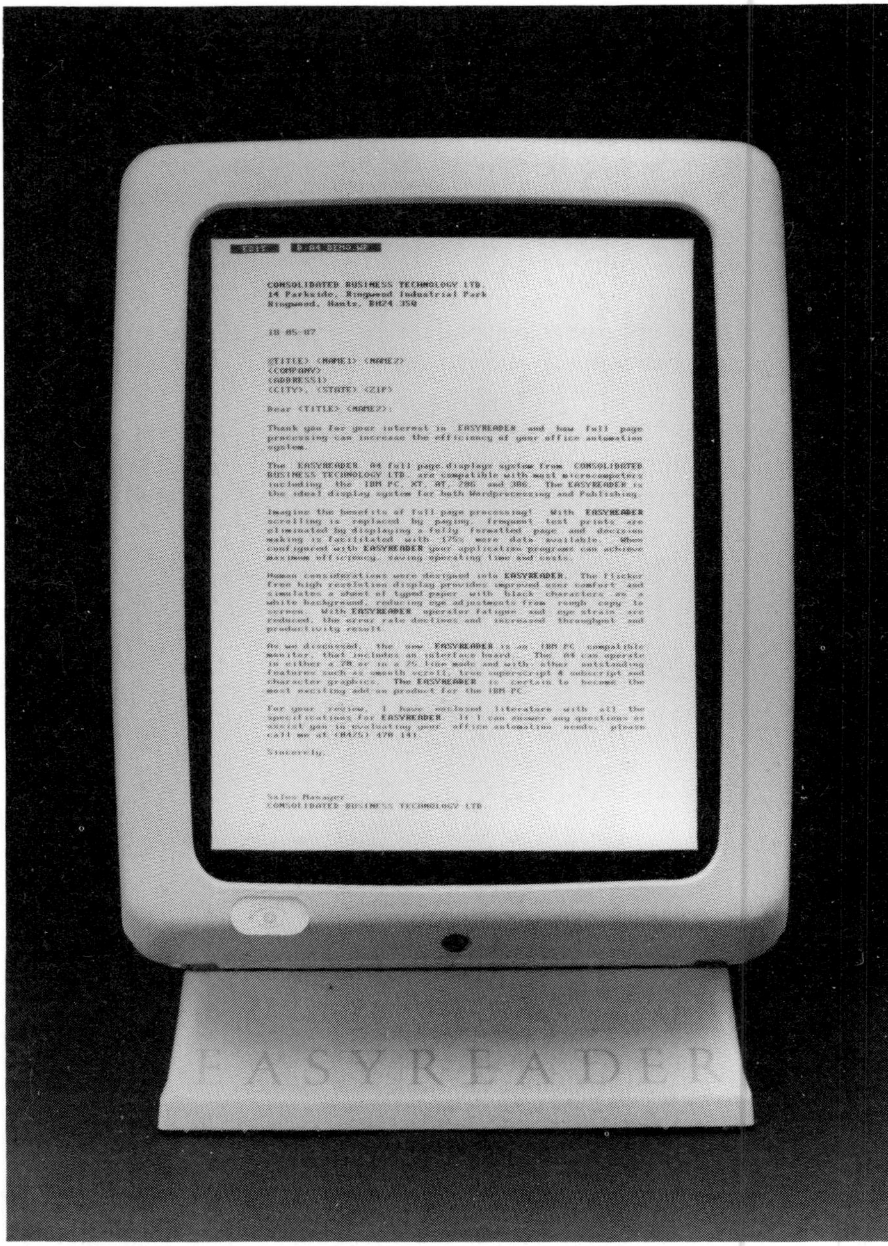

Easyreader screen with full A4 capacity

screens, with green text on a black background. Other options are amber on black (supposedly the most restful combination), white on black or 'paper' screens (black on white). Many monochrome monitors are able to represent colours as a variety of shades of grey, which is a great improvement on the single-shade models.

- *Colour* Colour monitors add a little variety to the dullest of displays. If you are going to use any sort of graphics in a serious way then it is hard to manage without colour though it can be done, and frequently is. The number of colours varies considerably.

Choosing between monochrome and colour is only half the story. You also need to decide how high a resolution you need. The *resolution* of the screen is a measure of the detail you can display. All screen displays are constructed from a grid of pixels, each of which may take any of the available colours. The more pixels there are, the higher the resolution and the better the display.

The resolution of any program's display is determined by three things: the quality of the monitor, any adapters that are attached and the software. Adapters are cards that are either fitted in the machine when it is purchased or added later. There are a number of different adapters on the market, and they are being constantly improved upon. The most common terms you will encounter are:

- *Colour Graphics Adapter (CGA)* This adapter is necessary to produce colour displays, though the resolution is not generally particularly good.

- *Enhanced Graphics Adapter (EGA)* This adapter allows you to create high-resolution displays and makes the difference between 'chunky' and smooth lines.

- *Hercules Graphics Cards* These are a special make of card commonly fitted to IBMs and compatibles to provide very high resolution displays on monochrome screens. Colour versions are now also being produced.

Many computers are now supplied with high-resolution cards already installed as standard. For example the Amstrad PC1640 has an Enhanced Colour Display (ECD) that can emulate all of the cards described above.

However, no matter how good your display system may be it will not count for much if the software you run has not been written to take full advantage of its capabilities. When choosing the display type it is probably best to take as your starting point the requirements of the software you are considering. There is no point having expensive options you cannot use; similarly, you must be careful not to choose a system that cannot run your software. Graphics packages, in particular, often have minimum display requirements.

Keyboard and mouse

The traditional method of entering information into a computer has always been the keyboard. This is undoubtedly the oldest component of the computer, being based upon the QWERTY design that has been in use on typewriters for over a hundred years. The design of the keyboard may be the most easy for the practised user, with the most commonly used letters in the most accessible positions, but this still remains the weak link in the computer system.

Apricot keyboard

The transfer of ideas and data through this unnatural process is still a great hurdle to the acceptance of computers in many situations. However, until the arrival of genuine and flexible voice recognition, an advance that will create an even greater revolution in information technology but still seems well out of reach, we are stuck with the keyboard and its derivatives.

It should be noted at this point that a course in typing is well worthwhile for anyone who is going to come into regular contact with computer keyboards. The ability to touch-type cuts down the time spent entering information and also reduces the number of mistakes made. For this reason everyone should be encouraged to acquire the skill, something which, once learned, sets you in good stead for life.

There are some aids to the entry of information via the keyboard, including special additional keyboards for data entry and programs that allow you to reprogram the keyboard's special function keys so that they will perform tasks that are frequently used.

Also becoming more widely used is the *mouse*. This is a small device that is helpful in selecting options from lists or for moving around the screen. The mouse has a roller underneath it, he movement of which is translated into movement on the screen. Two or three buttons on the top are used to give simple instructions. Thus, if a list of instructions is displayed on the screen, one of these can be pointed to by moving the mouse so that the chosen item is highlighted or indicated in some other way; the option is selected by pressing one of the buttons.

This provides a more natural way of making selections of this sort, but is obviously limited in its application. When entering large amounts of text, for instance, it is frustrating to have to keep transferring to the mouse to carry out operations such as saving text or marking out italic sections. The use of a

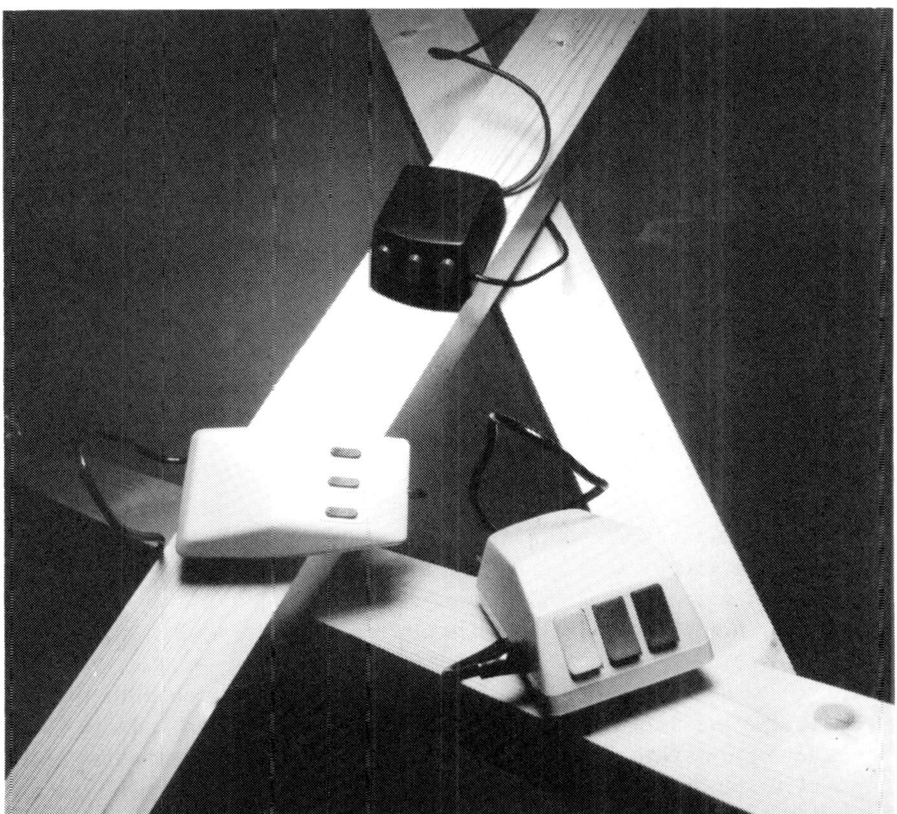

Various types of mouse

mouse is thus most convenient when keyboard input can be kept to a minimum, for example when carrying out disk housekeeping tasks, as described in Chapter 4.

Portable computers

Ever since the first microcomputers went on sale, manufacturers have been trying to design computers that are truly portable and then trying to persuade us that we need them. Sadly, they have, generally speaking, failed on both accounts. The so-called portables that have come onto the market have generally failed to pass the portable tests of being light, compact, easy to pack away, robust and not prohibitively expensive.

An example of this failure must surely be the Apple IIc. There is no doubt that this was an excellent microcomputer – still widely used in many offices - with reasonable memory (for its time), crisp display, reliable disk units and a good range of software. However, portable it certainly was not (in the true sense of being a complete portable system, that is). The main microcomputer itself was very carefully and cleverly designed, very light with a built-in keyboard and disk drive and a carrying handle that doubled as a stand to set the keyboard at a comfortable angle. But a system unit alone is not enough. A monitor is also essential, and the additional stand that came with it was very heavy, not to mention the separate power supply and the external second disk unit, without which many applications were tedious to run, to say the least. Thus the 'portable' system required at least four bulky components, let alone the packs of disks and other essential accessories.

One of the problems of portables is the display. The standard monitor is bulky because of its cathode-ray tube. Many portables get around this problem by incorporating a flat-screen liquid crystal display (LCD) that can fold down: the disadvantage is that these screens can be difficult and tiring to read, especially for long periods.

Perhaps the main reason for the failure of portables to make their mark is that most of us don't really need them. How often does the average computer user desperately need the services of a micro when they are out of the office? How many of us want to take 'taking work home' to these extremes?

There are some lines of business where a portable can be effective; for example, an insurance salesman can produce quotations rapidly while discussing options with the customer. This avoids delay, makes the task of the salesman easier and ensures that both parties are fully aware of what is being considered, so reducing future misunderstandings. If you do need a portable, then Olivetti, Hewlett-Packard and Victor are well worth considering.

The Toshiba T3100/20 desktop portable AT has an internal 20-megabyte hard disk drive

The Amstrad PPC640 portable computer

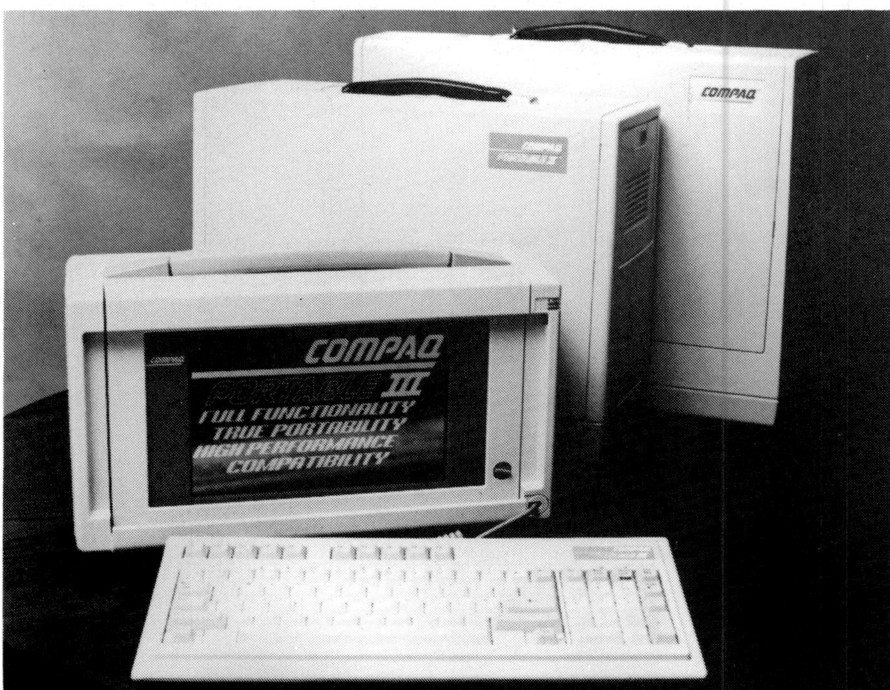

Compaq portable computers

A portable computer used as a terminal on a cellular telephone network

Where there has been success it is in those situations where the portable does not aim to take the facilities of the office to an outside location, but aims to solve problems that cannot be brought back to an office. An example of this is the Husky Hunter, a small hand-held battery-powered computer with built-in display that is ideally suited to the collection of data from distant recording devices (for example, river levels, weather recording and traffic control). The aim is not to process the data on the spot but to bring it back to the office where it can be transferred to a standard micro.

Therefore if you are considering a portable you should ask whether it is really necessary and, if so, whether the job is not best done by a machine dedicated to that particular task rather than one that attempts to be Jack of all trades.

Software

The hardware described above needs to be complemented by suitable *software* if it is going to be of any use. Software consists of the programs (the lists of instructions) that tell the computer what to do. A computer alone is nothing more than the raw materials from which to work. It is the software that converts these into a system that can perform some useful task.

With the right programs your computer can take on a number of different personalities: accountant, stock controller, personal secretary, graphic designer or playmate (if you enjoy computer games).

The most common categories of software are:

- *Word processors* These programs are dedicated to handling text. They are used to prepare any sort of letter, memo, report or that great novel you've always said you could write.
- *Databases* Computers love large amounts of data, especially if it all follows a common format. Database programs provide the means to manipulate this information into lists, reports and management schemes.
- *Spreadsheets* These programs allow you to store information on a grid and then perform calculations upon it. Perhaps the most typical example is that of the financial projection, where a set of figures can be entered and then worked upon until some satisfactory conclusion is reached.
- *Accounts* In many respects accounts packages are specialised database programs with the added facilities of the spreadsheet often thrown in. The company accounts are often the first task to be automated in the office.
- *Graphics* Information is much easier to comprehend if it is in a pictorial format, so the addition of a graphics package to a database, spreadsheet or accounts program can help in the interpretation of the results you produce.
- *Desktop publishing* Most recent arrival on the software scene, this category of products combines the text-handling abilities of the word processor, the more interesting capabilities of the graphics package and the latest advances in printing technology to create complete documents, often of typeset quality.

Each of these main categories is described in detail in the following chapter. Other ranges of software are described in Chapter 5, along with some of the integrated packages that aim to bring all these facilities together under a single umbrella program.

Chapter 4

Computer software and programming

This chapter looks at the software components of the computer system: its operating system, commercial programs and programming possibilities.

Operating systems

When choosing a computer, the operating system is not a feature you really need take into consideration, but it is something of which you should be aware.

Whenever you start up a computer its internal programs carry out various checks upon the hardware (in the case of the IBM, these take a tedious length of time to complete) and then these load from disk another set of programs, known as the *operating system*. The task of the operating system is to co-ordinate the activities of the computer until such time as an application program is put into effect.

For example, if you want to make a copy of a disk, move data from one disk to another or change the date and time as held by the computer, then these are all tasks that are carried out by utility programs under the control of the operating system.

The operating system's prime function is the supervision of the flow of data within the system, whether it is between the disk and printer, the disk and monitor or from one disk to another. As you will see, most activities relate to disks in one way or another and for this reason the system is often referred to as the 'disk operating system'.

The operating system has full control over the functioning of the computer right up until the moment when the application program takes over. It allows you to type the name of the program, checks that the program exists on the specified disk, loads it into memory and starts it running. If the program is reasonably well behaved you will be returned to the operating system as soon as the application is complete.

Resetting the computer

Some applications do not provide a means of getting out of the program and the only option is to start again from scratch. There are two or three ways of restarting a computer (if something has gone dreadfully wrong or a program will not let you quit):

- *Press the break key* You can often interrupt a program or some other operation by pressing a specific key. This may be a special Break key or a particular combination of keys (usually pressing Control and C simultaneously has the desired effect).

- *Operate the computer's reset procedure* This is a process whereby the computer's memory is cleared, the operating system is re-read from disk and you are left in an identical situation to when you first started. Note that all information in memory is lost, so this should be saved only for those occasions when all else fails.

  Resetting the computer is achieved either by pressing a carefully located switch (on the side of the Apricot keyboard or at the back of a Victor) or by pressing some obscure combination of keys (Apple-Control-Reset on the Apple II or Control-Alt-Delete on the IBM and its compatibles).

- *Switch off the computer and then switch it on again* This is not recommended if it can be avoided as it puts unnecessary strains upon the hardware. If you must do this – for example, if the computer refuses to be reset or you want to load a new operating system – then you should wait several seconds before turning on again to avoid any potentially damaging power surges. Save this option for occasions when nothing else will make the computer respond.

Operating system compatibility

When considering operating systems the question of compatibility once again rears its ugly head. Most computers rely heavily upon a single operating system. For example, MS-DOS is now widely accepted on large numbers of computers, appearing in several different versions. The version used specifically on the IBM PC is called PC-DOS. CP/M is an earlier operating system that is now fast disappearing. Apple tends to have its own operating systems, such as ProDOS.

The problem is that most programs are written to work with only one operating system; they are said to 'run under' the operating system. That means that you must have the correct system – and often the precise version number as well – for the program to operate correctly.

This is not generally a problem if you stick to programs that have been bought specifically for your model of computer, but if you try to use programs from other computers or transfer data to other systems you may come unstuck. For example a program designed to run under MS-DOS version 3.2 will not necessarily function with earlier versions such as 2.0.

When the Amstrad PC1512 was launched Digital Research attempted to overcome this problem by developing a system called DOS Plus, which was able to work with data and programs for both MS-DOS and CP/M. In the overwhelming majority of cases this system is a success. However, DOS Plus has been dropped from the Amstrad PC1640 because there is little CP/M software that can cope with the computer's enhanced graphics display.

As with anything else the secret is to keep in mind exactly what you want to do whenever you add any new component to the system, whether it is a new program or a new piece of hardware. Always satisfy yourself that there will be no problems before you make the final decision to buy. This all sounds rather daunting at first, but in fact you should find that you quickly acclimatise yourself to the peculiarities of your system and you soon learn what can and cannot be done.

Operating system techniques

The main problem with most operating systems is that they are rather archaic in the way that they function. User-friendliness is not a virtue that is readily associated with the operating systems that we all know and love.

Yet you are very dependent upon the operating system for many fundamental activities. Each selection of data is stored in a named *file*, as is each program or part of a program. You need to see what files are on each disk, and you need facilities to copy files, rename them and delete them as well as a whole host of other tasks.

Some of the better applications programs offer you the chance to copy and rename files, or even prepare new disks, but in the main it is expected that all this 'housekeeping' work will be done when you return to the operating system.

Systems such as MS-DOS still work largely on the principles of the old mainframe computers and their terminals. Although the conversation between operator and computer is now recorded on the screen rather than on the teletypewriter's paper, the instruction-response sequence is the same.

A symbol (the prompt) is displayed to indicate that the computer is ready for an instruction; you type the command and press the RETURN (or ENTER) key, the system carries out the instruction as best as it can, displaying suitable messages along the way, and then displays its prompt again when it is ready for further commands.

All this is done in a strictly linear fashion, with each new exchange appearing on the next line of the screen and the display scrolling upwards to provide more space at the bottom when the screen is full. All very functional, very tedious and very prone to error.

The instructions tend to be rather obscure and not always immediately obvious. For example, to delete all WordStar backup files from the disk in the right-hand drive (drive B) requires the command:

```
DEL B:*.BAK
```

This is one of the simpler commands. It looks terrifying to the new user, but once you become familiar with the way in which these commands are constructed it is surprising how quickly you become accustomed to effecting far more complex instructions. However, this is one area where improvements are being made and the future has a lot to offer.

Operating environments

In recent years new systems have started to appear. These have begun to offer a radically different approach to the whole business of giving the computer instructions, whether working in the operating system or within an application.

These new systems harness the opportunities provided by high-resolution graphics to create an environment based on pictorial representations, making the concepts they rely on far easier to grasp. Regrettably, these have come to be known as *WIMP* systems, standing for Windows, Icons, Mouse and Pointer:

- *Windows* Instead of treating the screen as a single entity a number of windows are placed on the display, as and when needed. Each window has a specific function: to show the results of calculations, to select from a group of files, to show the options available and so on. Windows may be placed side by side or, more usually, they overlap or are placed over the top of other windows. Thus they come to imitate pieces of paper piled upon a desk.

- *Icons* In WIMP systems text is kept to a minimum so files and disks are represented by small pictures called *icons*. Individual concepts may also have a graphic interpretation. For example, you will sometimes find icons for throwing files away (the dustbin or 'trash can') and for indicating that the machine is busy (an hourglass symbol in GEM, a bee on the Atari). From this you will have realised that most systems are designed in America and that their creators sometimes have a wicked sense of humour!

- *Mouse and Pointer* The handy little helpmate described earlier is the workhorse of these systems. A pointer, usually in the form of a small arrow, is placed on the screen. The movement of the mouse is directly related to the movement of this pointer. Move the mouse left and the pointer moves left, move the mouse away from you and the pointer obligingly climbs up the screen. Thus the mouse lets you point to a particular icon.

  The mouse buttons provide a surprising degree of flexibility in the instructions you can give. In Digital Research's GEM, for example, 'clicking' the button highlights a file to be renamed; 'double-clicking', i.e. pressing the button twice in quick succession, starts the program whose icon you are pointing at; 'dragging' the pointer, involving holding the button down while you move the mouse, results in an icon moving from one window to another and has the physical effect of copying a file from one disk to another.

The first of these systems to have any real impact appeared on the Apple Macintosh, where they have been put to very good effect and have attracted many fans. Not long afterwards remarkably similar systems appeared on the IBM range in the guise of Digital Research's GEM, so similar in fact that they were quickly followed by legal action, resulting in some subtle changes to the later version of GEM. (One casualty was the GEM trash can, which was no real loss, though its twin remains on the Macintosh.)

Other packages that provide a working environment of this nature include Microsoft's Windows and IBM Topview. These environments also have the advantage of providing *concurrency*, the ability to start one program and leave it running 'in the background' while you work on some other project.

These WIMPs thus act as intermediaries between the operating system and the user, provide a more fun way of dealing with the system and greatly reduce the need to resort to the old teletype commands. However, there are

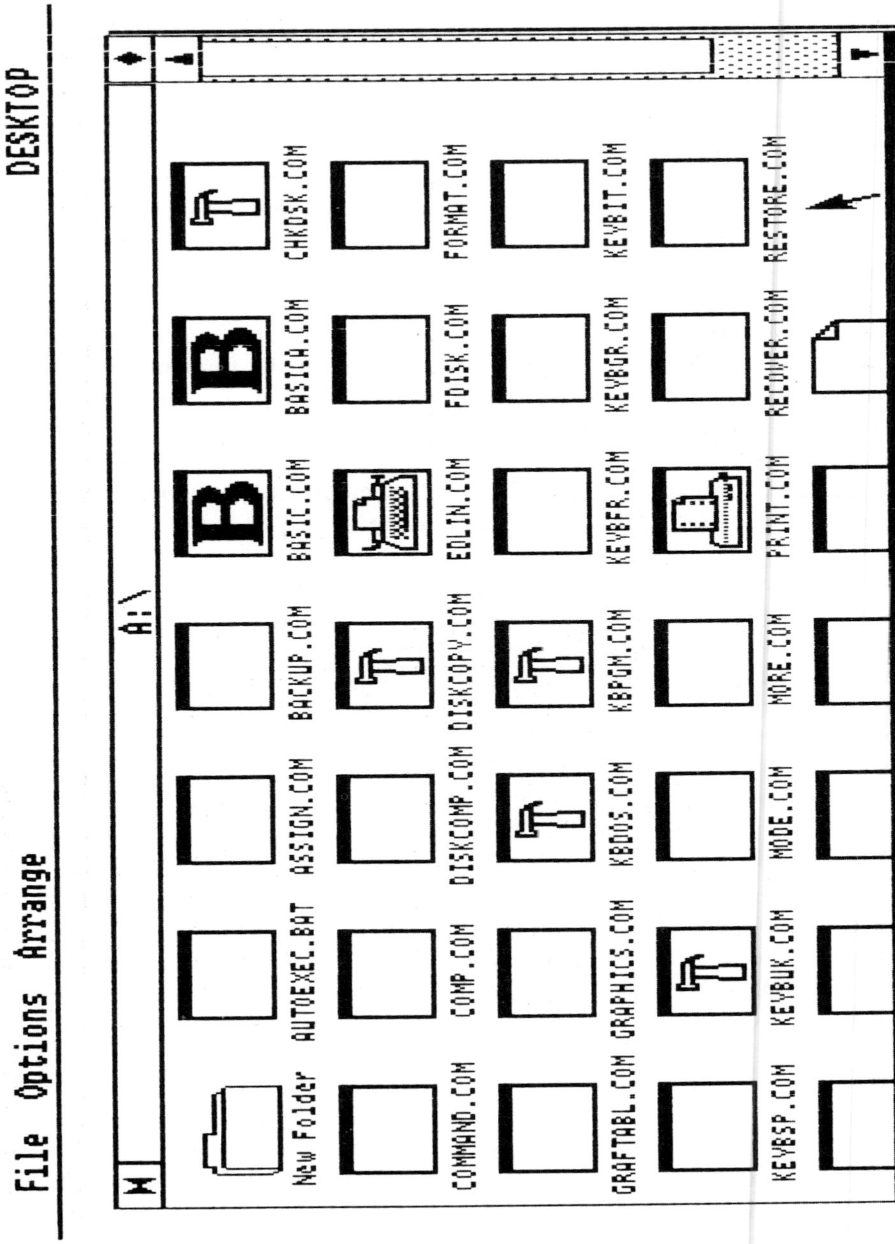

Files display with GEM Desktop

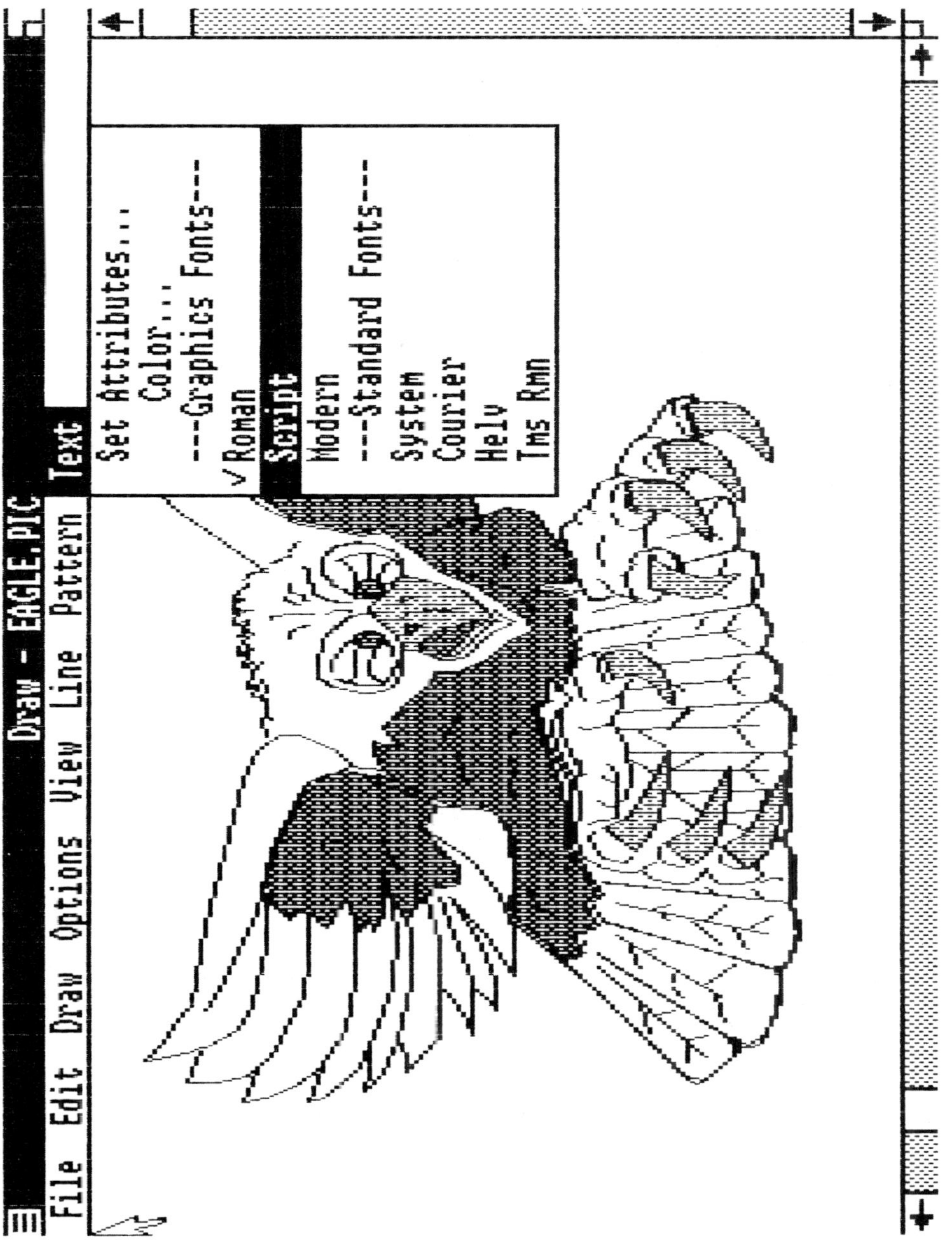

A Windows display with a drawing program

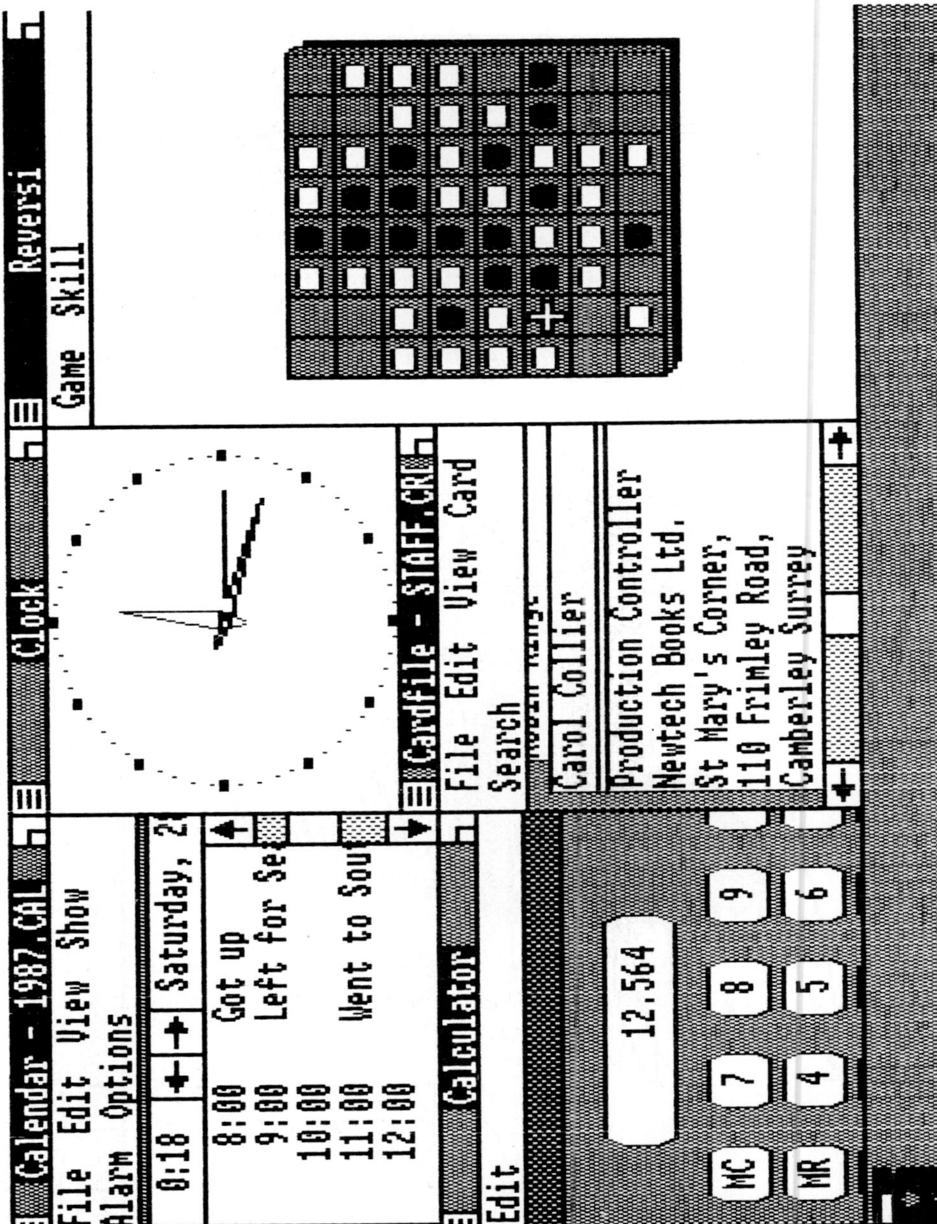

A Windows display with several windows open

still many concepts that are too complex for the systems to handle and we must await further developments before the workings of systems such as MS-DOS finally become totally invisible to us.

Applications software

The software that is available for any make of computer is extremely varied and covers a huge range of applications. In addition to the main categories of program described in the following chapters, there are a number of other programs to perform specific tasks:

- *Notepads* Programs such as Offix from Emergent Technology allow you simple text-handling facilities and memo-typing without the cumbersome nature of the word processor.

- *Diary and address book* Various 'desktop' programs incorporate these facilities, such as Quantec's QED which can actually dial the number for

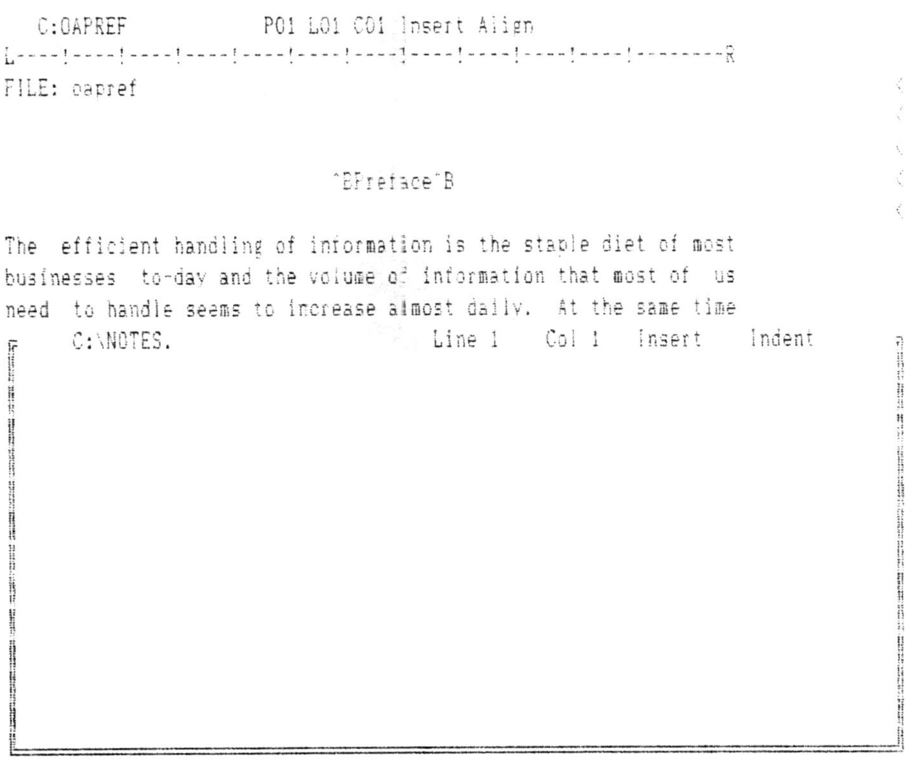

WordStar4 screen with Notepad from Borland's Sidekick overlaid

you (if you have a suitable modem). Many of these are 'background' programs (see below).

- *Reassigning keys* Programs such as Prokey and Smart Key let you define a long sequence of characters (for instance, an often repeated command) to a single key. Carefully selected, these keys will still operate in this new way even when you are running another program.

- *Background general purpose* Perhaps the most useful and easy-to-use programs are those that are loaded into memory when the computer is first switched on and then sit 'in the background' until needed. No matter what application you subsequently run (with a few exceptions) the background program's services can be put into effect by pressing a single key or combination of keys. These programs provide such facilities as a notepad, calculator, diary and address book. One of the most common is Borland's SideKick, which is activated on the IBM by the combination of keys Ctrl & Alt.

```
                        WordStar Professional Release 4
=========================== O P E N I N G   M E N U ===========================
    D open a document                   L change logged drive/directory
    N open a nondocument                C protect a file
    P print a file                      E rename a file
    M merge print a file                O copy a file
    I index a document                  Y delete a file
    T table of contents     SideKick Main Menu   ectory off
    X exit WordStar                              d
    J help                  F1     Help          S command
                            F2     NotePad
DIRECTORY   Drive C:\WS4  2.6  F3     Calculator
 .1k BITS            2.5k BRAD F4     caLendar              .4k CAVES
6.1k CHOIR            .4k COLL F5     Dialer         C     1.0k GIGI
8.3k LASER1.DOC      3.1k LASE F6     Ascii-table          1.6k LAWRENCE.BAK
6.1k MUSIC           6.0k MUSI F7     Setup          T     5.5k PRINT.TST
1.1k RCSTAT           94k READ Esc    exit                  .9k RULER.DOC
 .6k SAMPLE1.DOC      .4k SAMP                   DOC        .9k TABLE.DOC
5.5k TEXT.DOC        1.1k TRANICON      1.8k WS3KEYS.PAT   1.5k WSINDEX.XCL
```

WordStar4 screen with Sidekick main menu overlaid

- *Intelligent systems* These are programs that are able to learn from the user. A great deal of work is being done in this field, but is still very early days. There are some intelligent systems around but these are still highly specialised and very expensive.

Graphics programs

It is perhaps not surprising that the manipulation of volumes of data still dominates computer software. First, it is the speed with which computers can perform calculations and comparisons that makes them so remarkable and so vital to the office. But secondly, the computer, being based upon a grid-based form of representation in its displays, its printouts and its memory, is unsuited to realistic and detailed representations of the real world. Any attempts to produce pictorial results give only an approximation of the real object that is under consideration. Therefore, although it is possible to produce graphic representations quite rapidly, these are often unsatisfactory when compared to more traditional options.

Nevertheless, things are changing fast and the clarity of computer displays is improving all the time. There are also many applications where the graphics produced by computer are of a sufficiently high quality, especially if you are prepared to pay the price.

Some categories of graphics package are:

Numerical representations Bar charts, pie charts and line graphs are an obvious choice for computerisation. The tables of numbers that computers

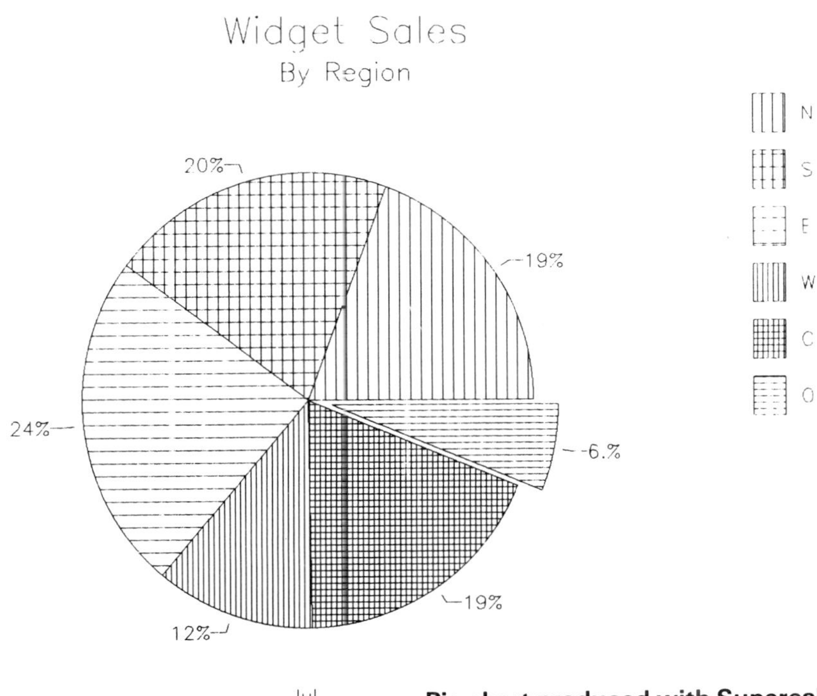

Pie chart produced with Supercalc3

love to produce are difficult to digest as raw data but can be transformed into something meaningful by conversion into some form of graph or chart. The peaks and troughs become immediately obvious, as do the comparisons of two parallel sets of data.

Programs vary from those that produce just the standard charts and line graphs to others with more exotic options. Psion, for example, offer three-dimensional bar charts as well as the normal two-dimensional options and allow you to combine graphs; two graphs called SALES and COSTS can be combined to form a third by entering the formula:

PROFIT = SALES – COSTS

Other packages offer less usual forms of representation. GEM Graph, for example, allows you to create symbol charts, where each 'bar' is made up from an appropriate column of symbols.

Painting programs This category of program tends to be used more for fun than for serious applications. Certainly programs such as GEM Paint (provided free with the Amstrad PC) can be used to embellish documents, but care has to be taken not to overdo it.

Computer Aided Design (CAD) Many drawing programs are available, ranging from the simple office accessories such as GEM Draw to highly specialised and technical suites for use by architects, engineers and designers. Needless to say these packages, and the hardware that is needed to go with them, are comparatively expensive.

Presentation graphics

A mention here should be given to the relatively small number of programs that are dedicated to the creation of text and graphics displays to aid a demonstration, exhibition or other similar occasion.

One of the leading 'popular' packages, i.e. at a price people can really afford, is the GEM suite of programs. GEM Graph, GEM Paint and GEM Draw have already been mentioned above; these can be linked to the GEM Write word processor and GEM WordChart. The latter is useful for creating the checklists and comparative charts that are so widely used in all forms of demonstration.

These individual programs can be combined together so that results from one can be passed to another (with a few exceptions). The resulting charts and documents can be output in a number of ways:

The GEM suite of applications programs

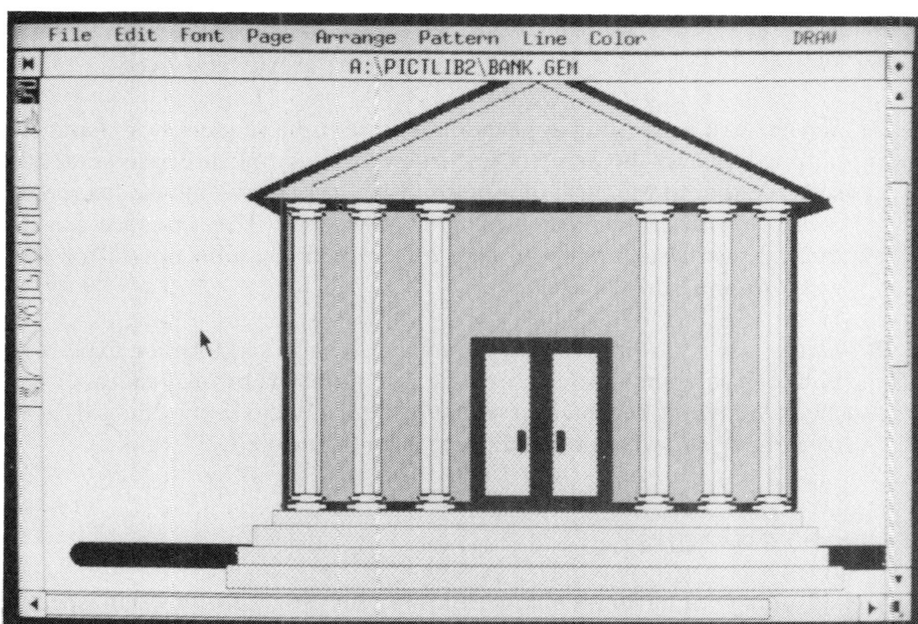

GEM Draw screen

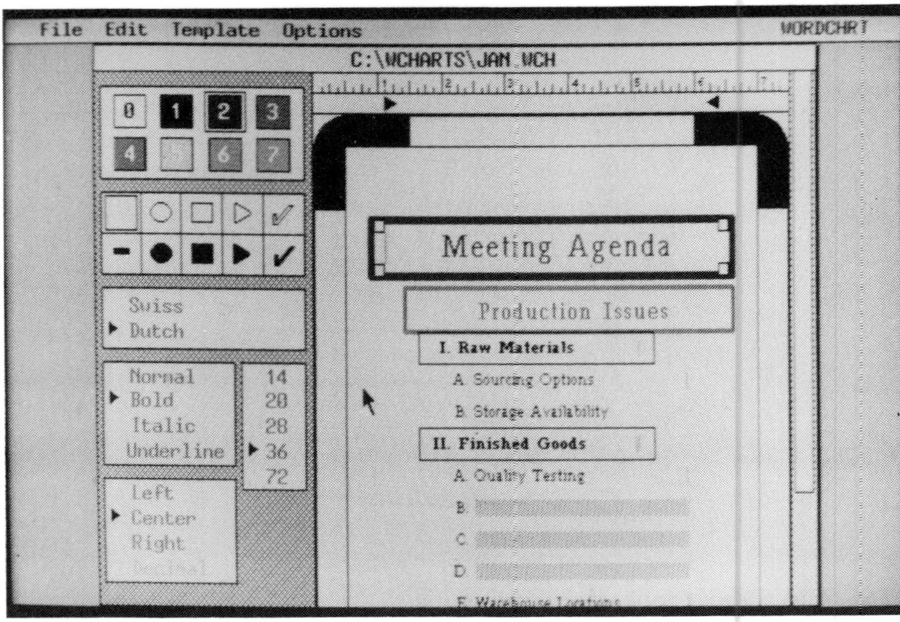

GEM WordChart screen

- *Laser printer* This is the most commonly used mode and provides a very basic form of desktop publishing.

- *Plotter* In this case the quality and detail are greatly improved.

- *Screen* An interesting application is to set up a sequence of charts and output them to the screen. Each new chart or picture pops onto the screen either at the push of a button (you can use the mouse for remote control) or after a specified number of seconds. The sequence can run through just once or repeat until interrupted, a useful option for shop windows and exhibitions.

- *Slides* By attaching your computer to special (and rather expensive) Polaroid equipment you can create and mount your own slides. It is at this stage that it becomes apparent how quickly the new technologies are converging and what potential there is for the future.

Integrated packages

The advantage of having a number of different programs for each aspect of business – word processing, database, spreadsheet, graphics and so on – is that you can pick the program with the best features for your needs in each

G5: +G3+G4 READY

	A	B	C	D	E	F	G	H
1		JAN	FEB	MAR	APR	MAY	JUN	
2	INCOME	--------	--------	--------	--------	--------	--------	
3	Sales	7500	7500	7500	7500	7500	7500	
4	Other	2000	1000	1500	1300	1000	1500	
5	Totals	9500	8500	9000	8800	8500	9000	
6	EXPENSES	--------	--------	--------	--------	--------	--------	
7	Wages	2000	2000	2500	2800	1800	2000	
8	Stock	2000	2000	2200	2500	2000	2000	
9	Rent	1000	1000	1000	1000	1000	1000	
10	Rates	200	200	200	200	200	250	
11	Fuel	250	200	300	280	240	180	
12	Other	1000	1200	1500	2000	1500	1600	
13	Totals	6450	6600	7700	8780	6740	7030	
14	--------	--------	--------	--------	--------	--------	--------	
15	B/F	10000	13050	14950	16250	16270	18030	
16	BALANCE	13050	14950	16250	16270	18030	20000	
17								
18								
19								
20								

04-Jun-87 03:32 AM

Lotus 1-2-3 screen

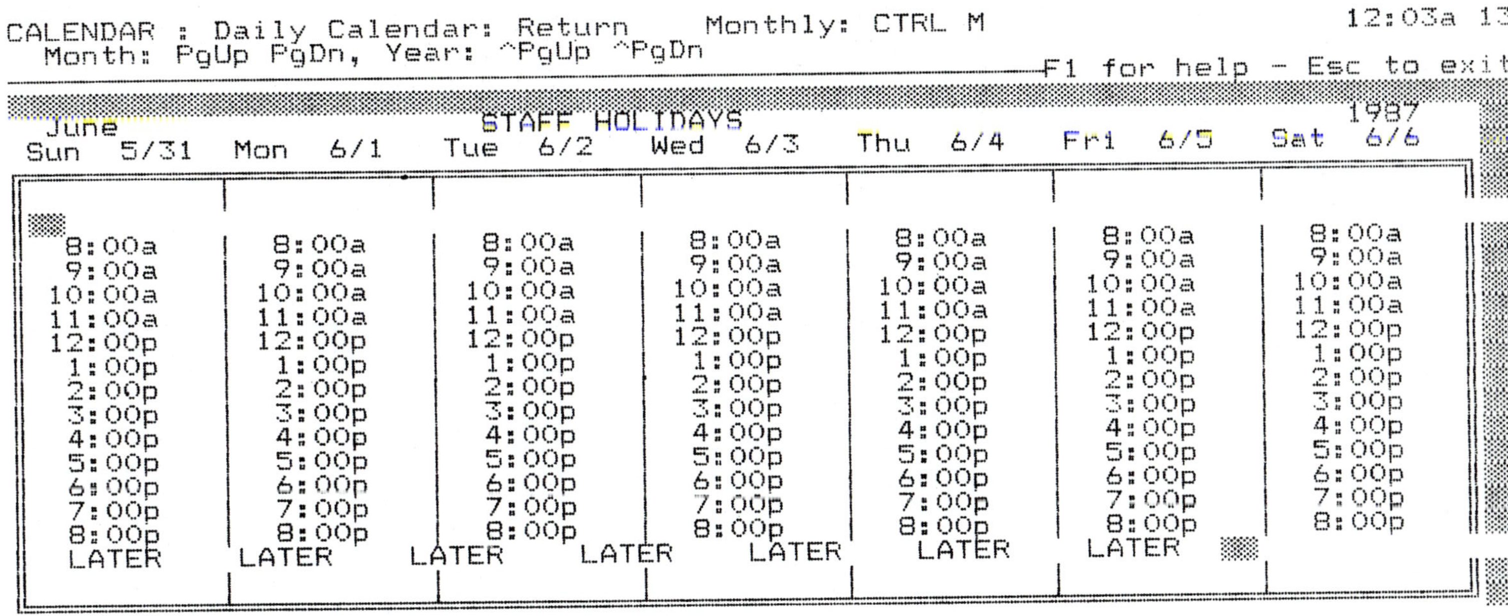

Sage DeskSet screen

case. Difficulties arise though when you need to use the results from one as the input for another. Sometimes it is possible, but you should always check the communication capabilities of pairs of programs before you buy.

Integrated packages over come this by supplying a set of three or more programs that can easily pass data between them. These packages fall into a number of categories:

- *Completely integrated packages*, such as Ashton-Tate's Framework and Symphony from Lotus, that allow you to show the results from two different programs on the screen at the same time, giving the potential to 'cut' data from one and 'paste' it onto the other.

- *Packages that are essentially a set of separate programs* linked through a main menu. Although you can only work in one program at a time in the case of Psion Xchange, for example, the work you are doing on others is still retained in memory.

- *Separate but compatible programs* that form a 'family', as is the case with the Perfect family and Microsoft's Word, File, Plan and Chart. The advantage is you need only buy those programs you need and can add others later. In all these cases you should look for ease of transfer between programs, common formats and commands and ease of movement between programs.

Programming

Inevitably there will be times when you want a job done, you know the computer can handle it, but there is no suitable software on the market. Alternatively, the software may exist but (as is often the case) does not perfectly match your needs. In some cases the differences may be slight enough for you not to worry (for example, a different format of invoice to that which you have used in the past). On other occasions there is a danger that you will end up adapting your activities to suit the program, perhaps getting a set of results you don't really need.

Since very few commercial companies offer a service to customise their programs to suit your needs you are left with two alternatives:

- *Write your own programs* This tends to require dedication and determination, as well as a great deal of time, but does ensure that the final program is really what you want.

- *Employ an independent programmer* This may be either an individual consultant if the job is not too large, or a software house for larger projects. Although you should get the product you need relatively quickly it will require a degree of supervision on your part and can also become very expensive.

Each of these options is described in further detail below. Perhaps the most important thing to remember, whatever option you choose – off the shelf, do-it-yourself or made to measure – is that the computer is there to improve your working practices. It should offer some form of enhancement, such as increased productivity, less expense, faster results, improved quality or better management. This means that sometimes a job is better done if it is not computerised, an option you should always keep in sight.

Writing your own programs

There can be great rewards from writing your own programs, if you are prepared to put in the time and effort that are needed. It is not just a question of sitting down at the computer and typing in instructions. Computers cannot understand English yet. They operate in languages of their own and to program completely you need to become fluent, but if the programs are to match the capabilities of the machine and are to optimise its features, then you need to attain a reasonably high standard.

Before embarking on this course of action you should satisfy yourself that the program hasn't already been produced in sufficiently close form for you to be able to adapt it for your needs. Most applications have been covered these days and you do not want to waste your time 'reinventing the wheel'.

The first task is to choose a suitable language. As stated earlier, computers converse in a machine code that consists of just zeros and ones. There is no need for you to come down to this level, however, which will come as a great relief to most potential programmers. There are a number of *high-level languages* that you can use. These come somewhat closer to English, with instructions such as:

```
IF TODAY$ = "24/08/87" THEN PRINT "HAPPY BIRTHDAY!"
```

The instructions are translated into code the computer can act upon in one of two ways:

- *Interpreters* These are programs that translate each instruction into machine code as and when it is needed. The disadvantage is that a section of code to be repeated must be translated each time, making the response much slower.

- *Compilers* In this case the whole program is converted into machine code before the program is run. This can be a lengthy process but the resulting program runs much faster.

The disadvantage of the compiler comes during the development stage, when a slight problem means you have to recompile again from scratch. This is frustrating and time-consuming. Often the best approach is to use the interpreter during the development stage and resort to the compiler when the program is almost complete.

Choosing the right programming language for a particular task is not easy. Each language has its own strengths and weaknesses:

Basic This is one of the oldest and most widely used languages. It was originally developed for beginners, but has come a long way since then. Although it is a flexible language that can be adapted to most applications – data handling, text manipulation and graphics – it is generally frowned upon by professionals and has never really gained respectability. Despite this, it is more than adequate for most needs and a very good starting point for learning programming skills.

A word of warning: Basic is not usually a *structured* language, though more recent versions do attempt to be. That is, you can jump to any part of the program with a GOTO statement, something that is not allowed in a structured language where the flow of the program is rigidly determined. Thus, if you intend to move on to other languages you would do well to learn the disciplines of structured programming and apply them in Basic where possible.

Newer versions of Basic remove the reliance upon line numbers that makes Basic so unmanageable for large programs and allow a more structured approach. Examples of this are MicroSoft's QuickBasic and Borland's TurboBasic.

Pascal This is a much more structured language that is often used to train programmers in their first language.

COBOL This language is widely used on mainframe computers and is particularly well-suited to applications involving large quantities of information and complex data structures. It is not very popular on microcomputers.

C This is one of the more recent languages, combining a structured approach with very compact programs and giving very fast results. It is becoming very popular for commercial programming.

There are a number of other languages available. Some of these are known as *Fourth-generation Languages* (or 4GLs). The aim of these is to make the task of programming easier. Examples include LISP, Prolog and a database-orientated language called PPlan2 from Farmplan Computer Systems.

Customised programs

Writing your own programs gives you complete and absolute control over the end result. However, very few people have the time to learn the skills that are necessary to produce a really good product that is totally free of errors (or 'bugs') and works fast and efficiently.

Therefore the alternative is to commission a software house or freelance programmer to do the job for you. This is undoubtedly the most expensive option, since you are paying for the full development costs of the program and writing even a short program can take a surprisingly long time. For this reason this option should be the last resort, used only when you cannot buy a suitable commercial program that can be modified to your needs. However, it does mean that you have ultimate control of what the program aims to achieve and for this reason alone can be well worth the extra investment.

When agreeing a contract for *bespoke software* (as these programs are sometimes called), you should include the following:

- *Specification* Who is to provide the details of what the program is to do and how it will be achieved?

- *Aims of the program* Make sure the programmers are fully aware of what you want to achieve with the program, what data it must use and how it should be affected by the program. Remember that the programmers cannot hope to make the program deal with situations that they do not know about.

  It is often the extreme situations that cause the most trouble: for example, a regular customer paying off all he owes you yet still getting regular statements and – even worse – menacing letters demanding that the amount £0.00 be paid within seven days! This sort of thing can lose you friends; sometimes it is the result of sloppy programming, sometimes the effect of a poor specification. In any dealings with computers attention to detail is very important.

- *Limitations* Similarly, the programmers should make you aware of any limitations of the program: situations it cannot deal with or that would be expensive to account for.

- *Documentation* How user-friendly will the program be? What level of documentation will be provided: a few simple operating instructions or a full manual covering all aspects of the program? Remember that a hefty manual will add an equally hefty sum to the final cost.

- *Timetable* Development time for programs is notoriously difficult to estimate, so you should not expect to be too hard on the programmers. However, you should agree a timetable and try to stick to it. This should include times for the presentation of the initial specification, the first mock-ups of the screen displays and data entry procedures, completion of individual sections of the program, full debugging with test data (which you will be expected to provide) and documentation. At each stage you should be able to inspect the progress and verify that the program is in line with the initial specification. If the timetable falls by the wayside it should not adversely affect the final cost; in some cases it is reasonable for the programmers to receive a bonus for early delivery or to incur penalties for late completion.

- *Price* Obviously you will agree a price for the product, but make sure you know what is included; as well as the initial cost of the programming you should agree whether it contains documentation, installation (the initial setting up of your system), training and – perhaps most important – later modifications. Inevitably, no matter how well the program is written, there will be bugs; the programmer should be prepared to correct these free of charge, but any subsequent improvements you ask for will certainly cost you extra. If you ask for any modifications during the development stage, make sure you know how much it will add to the cost.

- *Ownership* Who will own the copyright to the finished program? Will the programmers be entitled to sell versions of the program to other customers with similar needs and, if so, will you receive a royalty?

If you are careful about the way in which the initial agreement is drawn up and you have received satisfactory references for the programmers, you can hope to get a program tailored to your business that ensures that you are in control of the computer, and not the reverse.

Program generators can sometimes be a useful compromise. These are packages to which you supply all the details of the program you want to create and the package then completes the process by generating the necessary code, with varying degrees of success. For example, Sycero by System-C generates Basic code that can be interpreted or compiled.

Chapter 5

Computer peripherals and accessories

There are a number of peripheral devices that can be connected to the computer system. Some of these are described below.

Printers

Whatever program you are using, almost without exception, an important part of the process will undoubtedly be the production of the results of your labours in printed form.

Unlike typewriters, telex and facsimile machines, in which the means to print out their results is built into the piece of equipment, computers require a separate printer. There are many different types of printer and your choice will depend upon the quality required and the price you are prepared to pay. Varieties of printer include the following:

Dot matrix These are amongst the cheapest printers available, and their quality can be correspondingly low. Each character is produced from a grid of dots (hence the name), in much the same way that characters on the screen are built up from grids of pixels. The dots are created by wires fired at a carbon ribbon. This sort of printer is ideal for internal office work, in that it is fast and cheap to operate. However, the quality is often too poor for the finished product.

Dot-matrix printers come in two basic types: graphics and non-graphics. The non-graphics variety can only print straight text. Any attempts to print graphics displays results in a confusion of block graphics characters being spread over the paper. All such work must be left to the graphics printer.

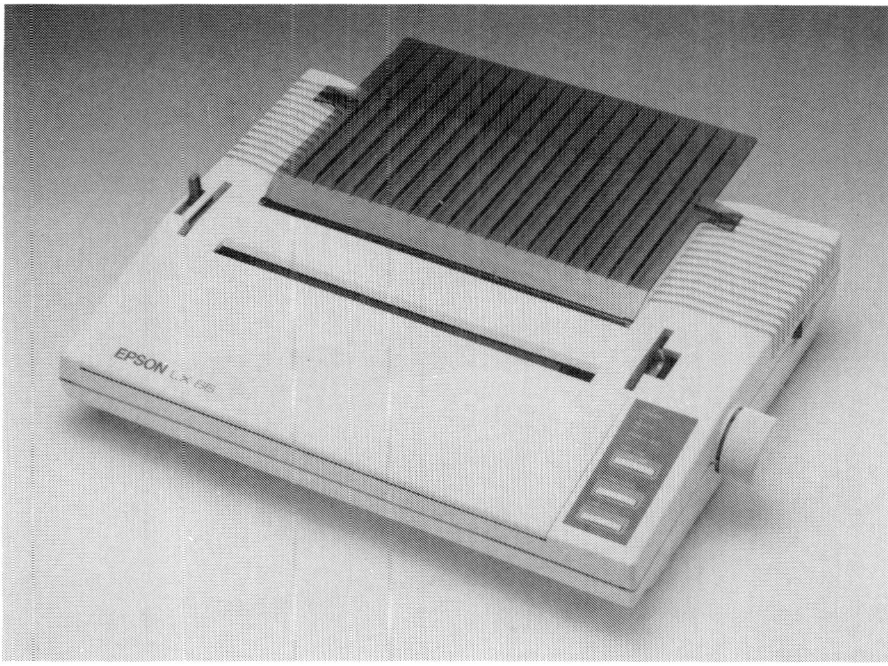

Epson LX-86 dot-matrix printer

The effect of the output from graphics programs in particular is often enhanced by the use of colour. Colour graphics printers are more expensive, but if you intend to use them for the finished product the extra expense can be well justified.

One of the leading manufacturers is Epson, whose machines range from cheap fast printers to the more expensive, but better quality, *near letter quality (NLQ)* printers.

Daisywheel It is frequently claimed that this range of printers is about to become obsolete as the laser printer revolution takes hold. However, until the latter come down to a competitive price it is likely that daisywheel printers will continue to sell in quantity. The daisywheel works in an identical way to electric daisywheel typewriters: a number of spokes radiate from the centre of the wheel, each containing a single character; to print the character the wheel is spun to the appropriate position and then the character is struck against the ribbon.

Daisywheel printers are more expensive than dot matrix but the quality is greatly improved and, since the daisywheels are interchangeable, they are capable of producing a variety of typefaces and styles. The drawbacks of daisywheel printers are that they can be very slow and exceptionally noisy.

Brother HR-40 daisywheel printer

Thermal printers Though widely used in the early days of the microcomputer age the popularity of this range of printers has waned in recent years. The printers produce their images by using heat-sensitive paper. This has the advantage of speed and very quiet operation but the great disadvantage is that special paper has to be used. Desktop calculators often have built-in thermal printers, as do some cash registers.

Ink jet printers These printers operate by squirting tiny jets of ink at the paper, producing an effect somewhere between the dot matrix and daisywheel. They have never proved particularly popular and are likely to be rapidly eclipsed by the laser printer.

Laser printers These are definitely at the top of the range, not only for quality and speed, but also in price. Although the price of laser printers has come down quite considerably since they first became widely available, they are still beyond the means of most businesses. Their price will undoubtedly continue to fall over the next couple of years, though.

Contrary to popular belief, laser printers do not operate by burning images onto the paper! In fact the technology is not dissimilar to that of modern photocopiers.

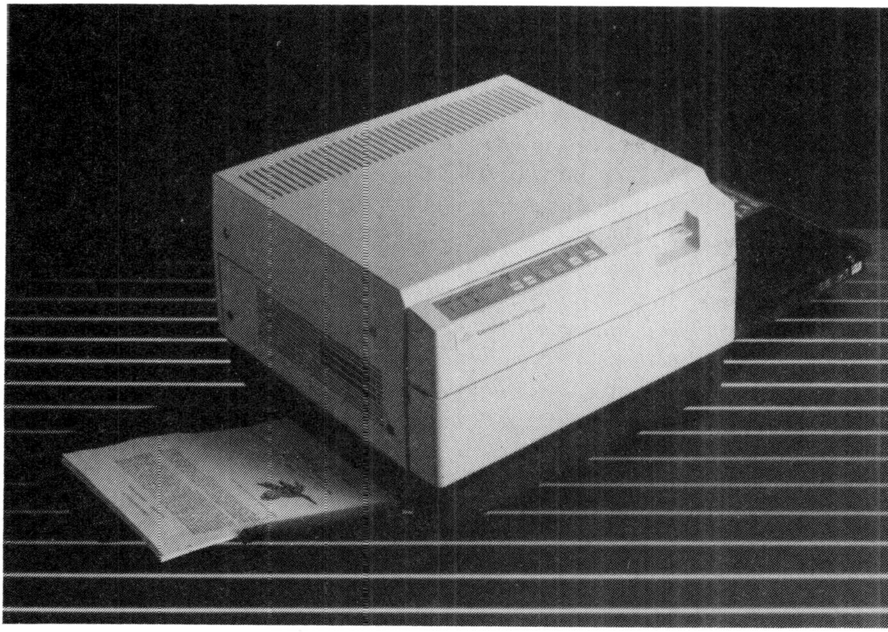

Centronics PagePrinter 8 laser printer

The price is justified by the quality of the result. Characters are very finely drawn and extremely clear, and, with the right software, even computer graphics can almost completely lose their 'dotty' effect. The added incentive is that the machines are almost totally silent, a tremendous step forward from the noisy dot-matrix and daisywheel printers.

There are also disadvantages. The main problem is that it is far harder to create the necessary communications link between computer and printer. The printer uses a special internal language, called a *page description language*, to determine the layout of the page and the computer software must be able to convert its output to this format. As a result, when choosing any piece of software you are often limited in the printer you can use. More than ever, it is essential to satisfy yourself that the printer will function satisfactorily with the rest of your set-up before you finalise the purchase.

Add-ons

As well as the standard components of the computer system – system unit, monitor, keyboard, mouse and printer – there are any number of extra devices that can be added at a later stage:

Standalone disk drives Whatever configuration you choose for your computer system you may well find that the disk drives are insufficient for your needs. The operating system can access more than the usual two drives and therefore one of the simplest ways of upgrading the system is to buy separate disk units. These may be hard disk units, to multiply your total disk capacity, or floppy drives to provide the option to read other disk formats; for example, a 3½-inch microfloppy unit may be attached to the standard IBM-compatible.

Tape streamers Backing up a hard disk is quite a headache. The smallest 10M hard disk requires 29 floppies, if it is full. The time taken to back up a 40M hard disk makes it almost impractical, apart from the tedium involved in swapping (115 floppy disks) every couple of minutes. However, hard disks do develop faults on very rare (and totally unexpected) occasions, so unless you back up important files to floppy whenever they are changed, this process is one that you cannot avoid.

One answer is to use a tape streamer, a device that will copy the entire contents of a hard disk to tape in just a few minutes. These devices are used

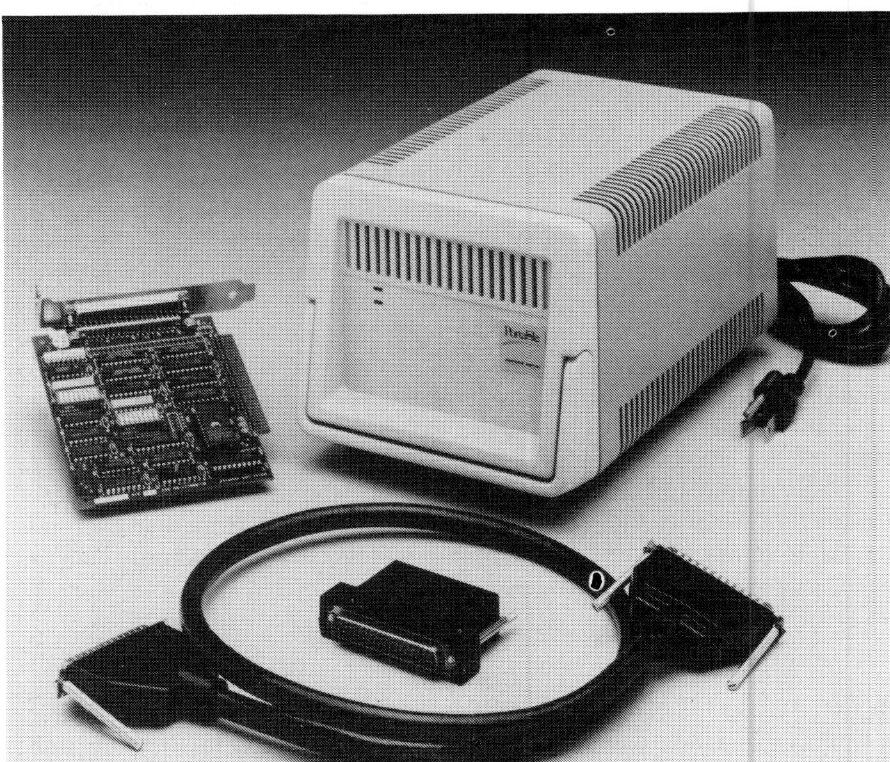

Western Digital Portafile portable data storage system

for security only, the entire contents being read back to hard disk in the event of failure; it is not feasible just to read a single file from tape. They also provide the means to transfer the contents of a hard disk to another machine.

Data cartridges An improvement on tape streamers, the data cartridge is faster and more reliable, with the ability to store very large quantities of data.

8087 maths co-processor Even the microcomputer, with its speed and versatility increasing annually, can sometimes seem slow (by comparison with our advancing expectations, rather than the computers of a few years ago). This is particularly the case when dealing with calculations involving large volumes of data. Performance can be greatly enhanced in such circumstances by the addition of an 8087 maths co-processor chip. This is a separate microprocessor, dedicated to the task of performing calculations, which leaves the main microprocessor free for its other tasks.

Graphics cards The addition of graphics cards (circuit boards slotted in internally) can greatly enhance the computer's display. The most commonly available are the EGA (Enhanced Graphics Adaptor) and the Hercules graphics cards, now with colour versions available. These cards increase the resolution of the screen, making the resultant display more clearly defined

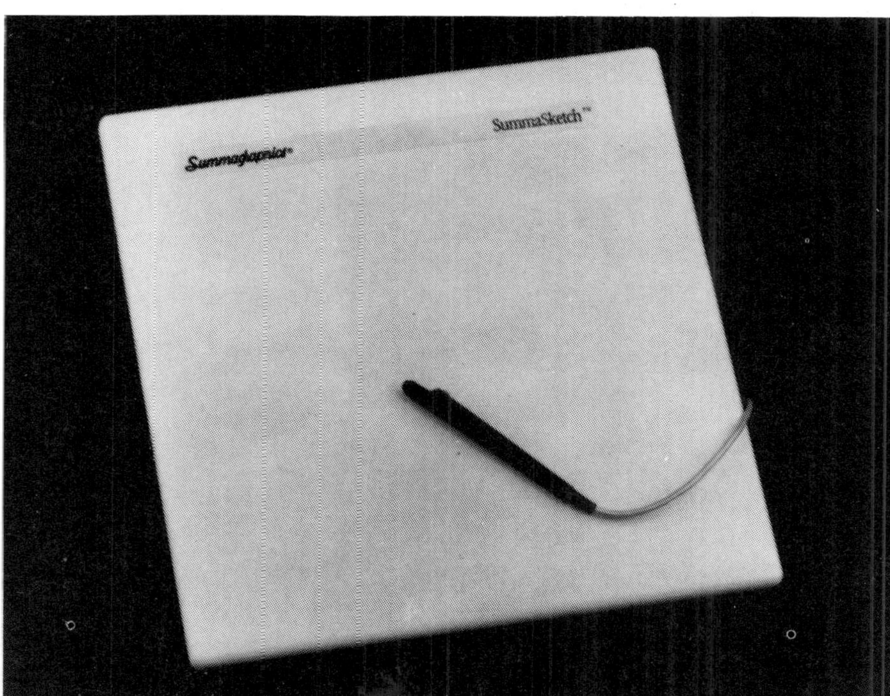

A graphics tablet – the Summasketch

and finely drawn. However, to make any use of such capabilities you must have software that can take advantage of them.

Graphics tablets These add-ons provide a novel means of entering data. The 'tablet' consists of a surface, marked out with a grid, that is sensitive to pressure. By pressing on the surface the co-ordinates of the point where the pressure is applied are transmitted to the computer. A suitably prepared program can make use of the figures supplied in the same way as if they had been entered at the keyboard.

Light pens This is another alternative form of data entry, with a similar effect to that of the mouse, but faster and even more natural to use.

Plotters Graph plotters are ideal for producing high-resolution graphics output. Far more accurate representations can be achieved than with traditional graphics printers as these do not have to resort to the use of dots, which bedevils many other forms of representation. Lines are straight and accurate, even when at angles. Most plotters offer a choice of different coloured pens, which can either be swapped part of the way through the plot or are automatically selected as needed. The drawback is that this more complex device requires special software to run it.

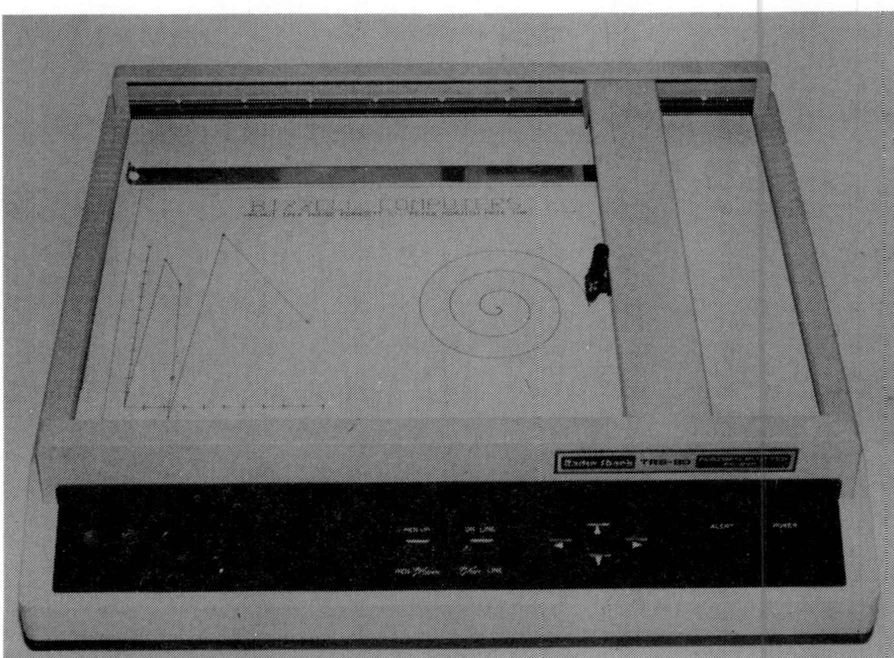

Radio Shack flat-bed plotter

Hewlett-Packard DraftPro plotter

Networks and multi-user systems

If you have a number of microcomputers along with a collection of peripherals, such as printers and plotters, then you may want to share these resources around the office and make the total capabilities of the system available to all users. Swapping disks between computers and pushing printers around on trolleys can become impractical. There are two basic ways of linking your computer equipment together:

- *Networks* In this case each of the individual computers retains its own independence but has access to the peripherals and a central hard disk unit.

- *Multi-user systems* In the multi-user systems the complete setup is based around a single powerful microcomputer, with a number of lesser terminals connected to it. Each terminal has access to the programs and data stored at the centre. To operate these you need a multi-user operating system such as Unix and true multi-user software. It has to be said that this area of computer development is still undergoing teething problems.

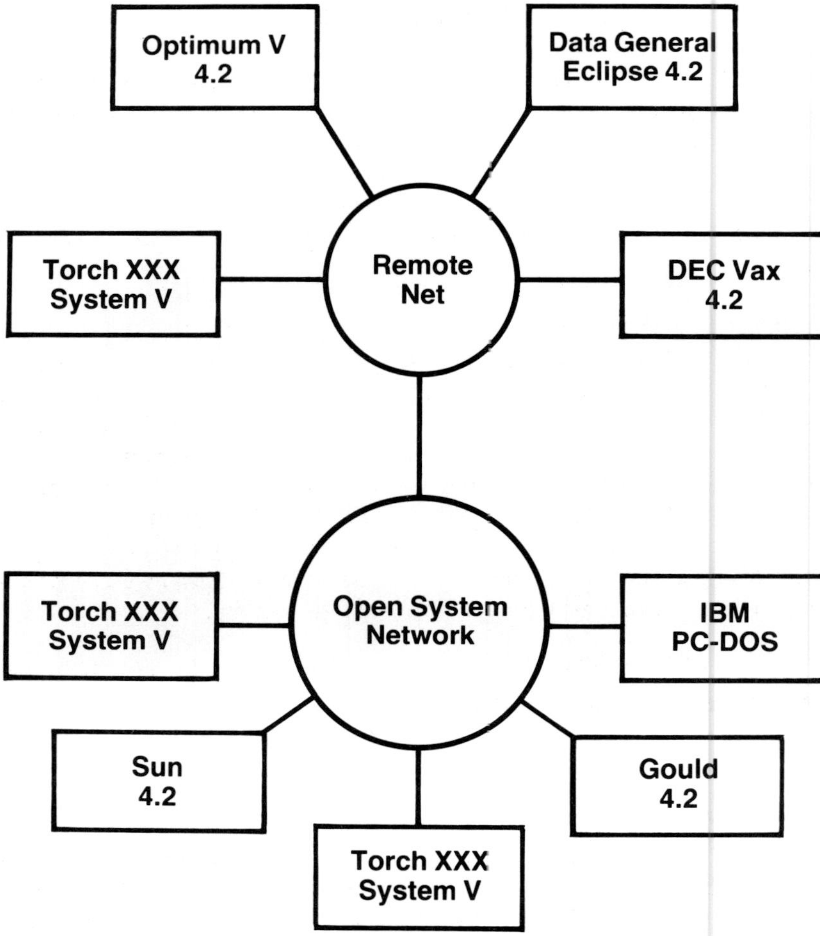

Network file system using the Torch NFS workstation

Networks may take one of two basic designs:

- *Star networks*, where all parts of the system are linked into a central file server that also routes data to printers and plotters where appropriate.
- *Bus networks*, where each computer is linked into a single communications line and data passes along the line until it reaches the appropriate point.

It is also possible to link in computers from outside the immediate office and surrounding areas through a modem and telephone link.

Consumables

Buying any new system is expensive, but the cost does not end there. You soon find that the computer has extravagant tastes. It has a voracious appetite for disks, paper and other 'consumables'. There are a number of mail order companies who deal in such products and once you have bought a computer or visited a computer show their catalogues miraculously start to drop through your letter box, along with a seemingly endless supply of computer magazines.

The mail order company may offer cheaper goods than your local dealer, but remember that they are harder to chase up if anything you order is defective. They have their reputations to keep so they will promptly replace any damaged goods, but it inevitably takes at least two days to make the replacement or place an initial order, even if they reply by return of post; a trip to your dealer can be accomplished in minutes. The mail order company will be able to offer a far greater range of products (for example, a choice of disk types), but you should set against this the goodwill you can build up with your dealer by using him regularly. The extra expense can be well worthwhile when you come up against a problem and need a little free advice.

Whatever you buy there will be choice, but you should soon learn from experience what particular product suits you best.

Disks

Even if you have a hard disk computer, you will get through a great many disks, especially if you keep permanent archives of original data. There are many different manufacturers and the price varies greatly. While not all cheap disks are poor quality, reliability is not always assured. Remember that your data is extremely valuable and expensive to replace. Cheap, unreliable disks could prove a very false economy. If you do choose cheaper disks, try to satisfy yourself that they are reliable by talking to a regular user; until you are happy with them, take plenty of extra backup copies.

When buying disks make sure you get the right specification for your computer, e.g. double-sided, double-density, 40 track, soft-sectored 5¼-inch; your computer manual or dealer will advise you. Most disks are very similar. The difference between single-and double-sided disks, for example, is that the manufacturer only guarantees the quality on one side of the disk. All disks start life as double-sided so you can use a single-sided disk in a double-sided drive; however, this is not advisable as errors are more likely to arise. Remember that it only takes one fault in a crucial part of the disk to make it unusable.

Note that the description 'double-sided' does *not* mean that a disk can be put in upside down (with the exception of the 3-inch disks used for the Amstrad PCW word processor). Double-sided drives have a read/write head for each side of the disk.

It can be useful to buy disks in different colours. Some manufacturers provide packs of disks of a chosen colour, others sell packs of ten disks in five colours. This is useful as long as everyone who uses the computer understands the system, e.g. red disks for accounts, brown for accounts backups, and so on.

Disks are extremely fragile and should be treated with great care. The 5¼-inch disks are most vulnerable. A few simple rules should be followed which are usually found on the back of each disk cover. In addition:

- *Never* use original program disks. Always make copies as soon as you buy any new software and work from the copies. Store originals and copies in different locations.

- Make *backup* disks (duplicates) of all data disks at regular intervals. The frequency depends upon how much data you are prepared to lose; if you backup only at the end of the day you can be sure the current disk you are working on will only get corrupted five minutes before you finish work!

- Keep *archive* copies of important data. For example, every month put a copy of the latest accounts disk into permanent storage, in a different location. Then at least the legendary cup of coffee tipped into the disk box will only set you back a few weeks.

Perhaps the most important point to stress is that disks are not to be trusted. Most of the time they work well, but you can guarantee they will let you down if you lower your guard. The fact that a disk has a 5-year guarantee is of little consolation if you have just lost your customer mailing list or the year's accounts. There are programs that will recover most of the data from a damaged disk (your dealer can probably do this for you), but you should not rely on them as the results are unpredictable.

Other consumables

You can spend a great deal of money on extras for the computer. Some is justified, much is not. Some of the products you might find useful include:

- *Quality paper* Computer paper is quite cheap so it can be worth the extra for higher quality, e.g. 80 gsm rather than the standard 60 gsm that sometimes resembles white greaseproof paper, or paper with micro perforations (here the outer edges containing the sprocket holes for the tractor feed and the separate sheets are divided by such fine perforations that the edges of the individual sheets are much smoother than is normally the case).

- *Labels* Continuous sheets of labels are a boon if you do regular mailshots, but make sure you get the size that matches the specifications of the program.

- *Drive cleaning kits* It is well worth using a kit from time to time to keep your drive heads clean, reduce wear and protect future data.

Accessories

Buying a computer is rather like buying a car. As soon as you start to use it you realise that there are plenty of optional extras that enhance its operation. The distinction between those that are essential, those that are genuinely useful and those whose main function is to use up the remnants of the office computer fund will depend on your particular business and the way you manage the office. Some that you might consider are:

Automatic sheet feeder This is a relatively expensive item of equipment that

Double-bin cut-sheet feeder for Epson LQ1500 printer with FIFO stacker

feeds individual sheets of paper into a daisywheel printer, as needed. It can be essential if you frequently need to print long documents, sets of accounts or other output covering many pages for which continuous stationery is not of high enough quality. The cost can soon be recovered if you would otherwise have to pay someone to stand over the printer and change the sheet every two minutes.

Acoustic hood Daisywheel printers make a tremendous amount of noise that quickly becomes unbearable even in large offices, if the printer is in continuous use. This can be cut down either with a normal printer cover or a more expensive acoustic hood. The level of noise from the average daisywheel printer is approximately 85 decibels; a normal sound cover can cut this to about 65 dB while an acoustic hood reduces it still further to about 45 dB. Bearing in mind that each increase of 10 decibels represents a doubling of the apparent noise level, acoustic hoods can provide some quite dramatic improvements in environment.

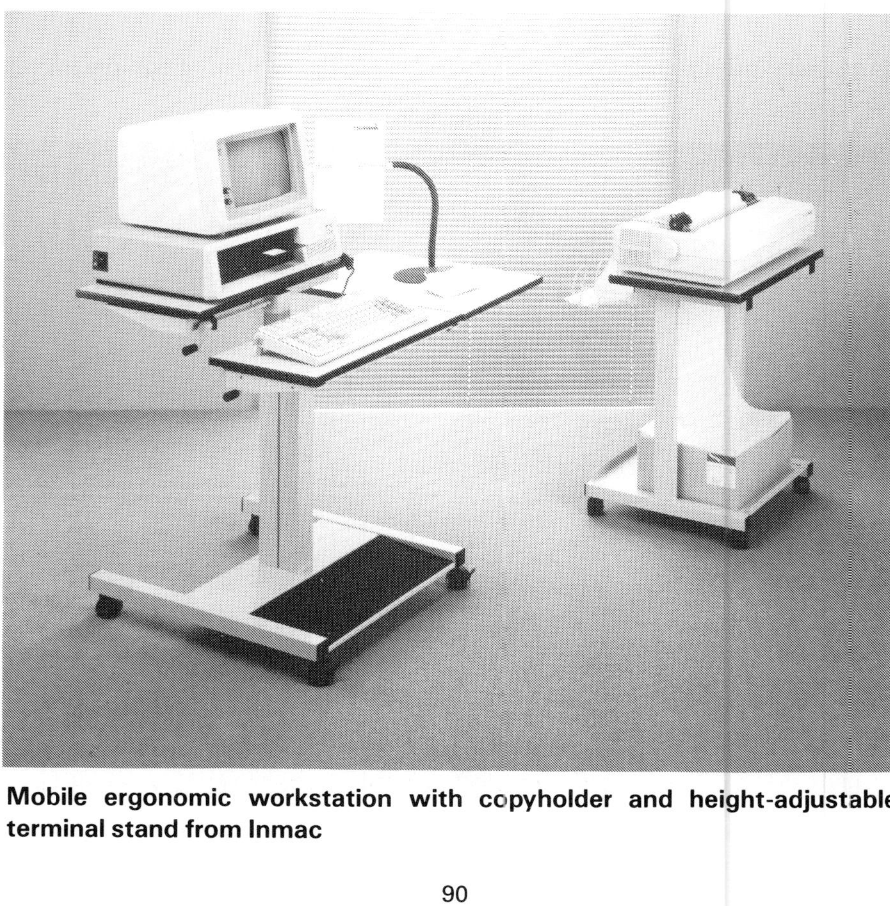

Mobile ergonomic workstation with copyholder and height-adjustable terminal stand from Inmac

Anti-glare screen filters Monitor screens can be difficult to read if they are in a position where the sun or office lights reflect off them. Some computers are supplied with anti-glare gauze fitted over the screen, e.g. some Apricots; for others you can purchase a clip-on filter.

Furniture Special desks and tables for computers and printers, at very special prices, are a luxury that most businesses cannot afford, but good chairs are essential for anyone working at a computer for long periods. Uncomfortable chairs and sitting hunched over a computer can cause backache, and other associated problems. However, a chair does not have to be a 'computer operator's chair' to be suitable!

Dust covers These are a very worthwhile investment for any computer or other piece of equipment.

Chapter 6

Word processing

As our offices produce more and more text, the ways in which we can manipulate this text become more and more important. Whether it is the production of a manuscript, the reproduction of standard documents or the printing of an envelope, it is important to have the right tool for the job.

The days of the humble typewriter, one of the earliest office automation devices, are undoubtedly drawing to a close, but nevertheless there is still a place for them in many offices. However, they are rapidly being replaced by both computers with word-processing abilities and dedicated word processors, often with computer facilities included. It is these machines that are discussed in this chapter.

Also important in this category are the devices that are used to prepare text for word processing, the dictation machines. Finally there is the revolutionary idea of desktop publishing, the new range of software and hardware combination that allows text and graphics to be welded together into a single, polished document.

Electronic typewriters

Electric typewriters of one sort or another have been around for many years, easing the task of typing and allowing much faster speeds to be reached by the competent typist. The latest breed of electronic typewriters is very different to their mechanical forerunners, providing far more than just the ability to impress a sequence of characters upon paper.

Canon AP800 series electronic typewriter

These machines are not computers, but nevertheless they often contain the same microprocessors that are the secret of the computer's success. In this case however, the circuits are dedicated to just a single function, the preparation of the printed word.

Features that you may expect to find in modern typewriters include:

- *Memory* Many typewriters now include their own memory for storing a limited amount of text. This means you can type a short document, and then let the typewriter retype it for you, if necessary making changes to the original as you go along, without starting again from scratch.

- *Speed* Although you are unlikely to be able to outpace the typewriter when entering text, the speed at which it recreates text in memory varies considerably. The Canon AP800 series can achieve speeds of up to 23 characters per second, for instance.

- *Justification and centring* Each line may be stored in memory until it extends beyond the right margin, at which stage it is printed out with extra spaces between words to pad them out so that the last word ends at the right-hand margin. Headings and other text can be automatically centred between the margins.

- *Emphasis* A choice of boldface, underlining, superscripts and subscripts may be offered. By exchanging the daisywheel that contains the characters you can swap to a completely new typestyle or size.

- *Background printing* Having entered and corrected one document, you may be able to type in another at the same time as the first one is printed.

- *Noise levels* The noise generated by typewriters varies considerably and is an important consideration, especially for small offices. The Canon AP800 Series are quieter than most.

- *Ribbon life* Ribbons are expensive, generally being packaged in special cassettes that do not allow the ribbons to be re-used. For this reason the number of characters printed per ribbon and the price of ribbons is an important factor when weighing up the costs.

- *Built-in screen* A display of the current text may be included, ranging from a single-line LCD display to a full 25- line screen.

- *Disk storage* The more exotic machines such as those at the top of the Canon range – offer the capability to connect to a floppy disk drive for storing text permanently. It is at this stage that you begin to wonder whether you have a typewriter or a fully fledged word processor. Other word-processing functions include spelling checkers and zoom options (to show the overall layout of the document or to home in on one area for editing).

This dazzling array of features makes the typewriter still a very respectable item for the automated office. There are some very significant advantages to the typewriter, not least the fact that there is no complicated and prolonged startup procedure if all you want to do is type an envelope.

Dedicated word processors

The next step up from the typewriter is the word processor. It handles text in the same way as typewriters, but with some fundamental differences. The principle of this category of machines is that the typing of the text and the printing of the document are two totally separate functions that are completed at different times.

A word processor is able to accept entry of text from the keyboard, but this is shown on the display screen rather than being printed out on paper. This text

Amstrad PCW 8256 word processor with letter-quality printer

can be stored away on disk for printing at a later time or held in memory and printed when complete.

The main advantage of dealing with text in this way is that it can be edited to remove any errors that may have occurred during the initial typing. A *cursor* is displayed on the screen to indicate the particular character under consideration and can be moved to any place in the text; the cursor takes the form of a flashing block or underline character. Any changes can be made to the text, new sections can be inserted and other blocks of text can be marked for moving to another position, copying to some other part of the document or deletion.

The initial text is only the raw material from which to work. Once the content is correct, the word processor provides a tremendous amount of control over the final appearance of the printed document, including various types of emphasis and formatting of the page.

When the document has been edited to your satisfaction, it can be printed out straight away, stored on disk for future printing and for reference or transferred to some other medium. For example, a document may be transmitted as electronic mail, thus removing the need to ever print the text on paper.

Perhaps most important, standard documents can be created and then adapted to suit each particular circumstance.

Many dedicated word processors include a variety of other computer facilities, just as many computers can be fitted with a comprehensive word-processing program. Indeed, it is becoming harder to tell where one stops and the other starts.

Most significant of the disguised computers in recent times has been the Amstrad PCW8256/8512 'word processor'. This is an fact an ordinary computer that has been sold with special emphasis on its word-processing capabilities. It was supplied with an excellent word-processing program from Locomotive Software and a printer was included as standard. For those interested in getting first-hand experience of word processing it proved an invaluable first step, especially if you were not too worried about the final quality of the printout. Although very good quality compared with most dot matrix printers, the output from the printer was obviously not up to the standards of a daisywheel printer.

These machines have now been eclipsed by the new range of Amstrad desktop computers and the recently launched PCW9512, a personal computer/word processor that is sold packaged with daisywheel printer that will accept paper up to 15 inches wide.

Computer word processing

The alternative to buying a dedicated word processor is to buy a computer and a word-processing program. This has the advantage that you can use the computer for all the other tasks around the office, such as accounts and databases. Indeed it is becoming harder, as word-processing programs become more sophisticated, to justify buying anything other than a desktop computer, especially now that you can get a full computer system and daisywheel printer for less than the price of a top-of-the-range electronic typewriter.

Another advantage is that if you buy a word-processing program and find that you cannot get on with it, but hear of something better, then it is quite cheap to change; choosing the wrong dedicated machine is an expensive mistake to be avoided.

The WordStar standard

The most widely used word-processing program is still probably Micropro's WordStar. This became the industry standard in the early days of word processing. As a result most people first learn WordStar, so WordStar becomes the obvious choice when anyone is thinking of buying a package. This remains the most popular program; yet another example of the success

The WordStar 2000 Plus package

spiral that has taken IBM, Amstrad, Sage Accounts and the dBase II database program to the top of the market and held them there. In many respects this is a shame because many very good products are overlooked simply because they are not popular, and never will be. (Having said that, most of the products that reach the top do so because they are good.)

It is WordStar that has brought us such gems as the Control-Y command to delete a line and Control-KK to mark the end of a block, commands that have been adopted by other programs (not only word processors) in an effort to maintain some sort of compatibility and to save the user having to learn another set of completely new commands. In this way these archaic commands have been perpetuated long after they should have been retired. Such commands are a throwback to the days when computers were short of memory and used only by expert computer operators, who were happy to work in languages and codes that bore little relation to the real world.

The 'WordStar diamond' is particularly widely used by other programs of all types. Control-E moves the cursor up one line and Control-X moves it down, while Control-S and Control-D move it left and right, respectively. This appears an arbitrary allocation of codes but a brief inspection of the keyboard layout shows that there is at least some logic to it.

There are several varieties of WordStar. It is now available, thankfully, in a greatly enhanced version, WordStar 2000, that makes use of windows and improved menu systems. A new, cheap and difficult to use version is also available for the Amstrads. And then, of course, there is still the original flavour for those who are hooked on it.

Word-processing programs can be expected to include all of the standard features you would expect to find on a dedicated machine:

- *Justification and centring* In the simplest form of justification each line is padded with spaces between the words so that there is a straight right-hand margin rather than a ragged one. Some packages offer a range of alternatives, such as a ragged left-hand margin and centring of all text about the mid-point.

- *Emphasis* Bold type, italics, underlining, superscripts and subscripts are all useful additions to make a document more attractive, if used sparingly. Remember that you must have a printer that can reproduce such features if they are to be any use to you!

- *Typeface* A few programs allow you to change the size and style of your text at different points throughout the document. Once again the main limitation is likely to be your printer.

- *Print pause* If you want to change your daisywheel to get a different typeface partway through the document then it is useful to be able to include an instruction to pause when printing within the text. WordStar offers this facility, but it is rarely found elsewhere.

- *Rapid jumps* If you are working with very long documents, then you need to be able to jump to a specific section without too much difficulty. This can be done either by placing a marker at some point in the document (as in WordStar) or by jumping to the top of a given page (Psion Quill, for example).

- *Search and replace* The greatest joy of using a word processor comes when you discover that you have consistently misspelled 'received' as 'recieved'. The search and replace facilities let you move the cursor to each successive occurrence of this item of text and, optionally, replace it with a corrected version.

  With a little cunning you can save yourself quite a lot of time; a long and complicated name, chemical formula or other item can be typed in as an abbreviation and then replaced throughout the document with the full version. However, it is always a good idea to use the search option on its own first to make sure that when 'pc' is replaced by 'personal computer', 'ripcord' does not become 'ripersonal computerord'! Computers have a knack of proving just how stupid they really are at the most inconvenient of times.

- *Block operations* Any section of text can be marked out for moving, copying or deletion. Very rarely you may be able to mark out blocks that do not cover the complete width of the text, so that you can move a column in a table from one position to another.

- *Page format* You should be able to specify the size of the margins at top and bottom of the sheet as well as at the sides. Provision is usually included to add headers and footers at the top and bottom of each page, with the option to include automatic page numbering.

In addition there are other features that may either be included in the program or accessed as extra programs:

- *Typewriter mode* Sometimes you do not want to go through all the motions of creating and saving permanent files. Programs such as Samna (from Thorn EMI) give you the ease of use of the typewriter with the editing and formatting facilities of the word processor.

- *Unusual characters* In some businesses the ability to produce characters from foreign languages and scientific symbols is essential. Vuwriter Scientific is a word processor program that incorporates Greek and scientific characters.

- *Mail merging* The most useful of these programs, and probably the most over-used, is the ability to merge a list of information with a standard document. For example, a list of names and addresses might be merged with a standard letter so that each copy would have the address of one person at the top and include their name within the letter itself. The items of data can usually be included more than once. Hence the letters that start "Dear Mr Morris," and continue a little later with "Yes, Mr Morris, it's true! You have been selected out of thousands of others ...." The original document probably included text in a format similar to:

  Dear &name&,
  Yes, &name&, it's true!

  Although this facility is greatly abused these days it does have some tremendous uses. If a list of customers' names and addresses also includes amounts outstanding then letters can be sent to all those who owe more than a certain amount, including the figure within the letter.

- *Spelling checkers* Programs that work through your document checking for errors can be a boon or a nightmare. They are ideal for a final check through to satisfy yourself that no typing errors have filtered through, but they will, of course, also pinpoint names, abbreviations and other words not in their internal dictionary. Generally you can add any frequently used words to the dictionary, but you may also have to add words such as 'colour' if it only recognises 'color'. The checker will not identify errors that result in another, correctly spelled word, for instance 'there' instead of 'their', or 'to' instead of 'too'. For these reasons it is important to see spelling checkers as a useful aid, but not a totally reliable one.

  Most programs insist that the checking is done only after the document has been saved on disk (as in the case of SpellStar, the companion of WordStar), while a few allow you to invoke the facility at any time, checking only from the current cursor position (for example, Microtrend's Trendtext/Expert).

- *Automatic indexing* Indexing of a long document can be a great chore. Therefore the ability to mark words that are to be automatically indexed is a significant advantage if much of your work includes this need. All the indexed words are put into alphabetical order and page numbers are added. Facilities vary dramatically, from those that only index actual words found in the text to others that will allow an occurrence of 'Granny Smith' to be indexed under 'Apples'.

- *Contents lists* Even easier to complete is a standard contents list, combining specified headings with their related page numbers and updating these if changes are made.

WYSIWYG – What You See Is What You Get

In line with the trend towards user-friendliness in all aspects of computer operation, the way the document appears on the screen can make a significant difference to how pleasant the word processor is to use. For example, the original version of WordStar, still in very wide use, indicates that a document is to be in bold type by placing the symbols ^B – by keying Control-PB – immediately before and after the emphasised section (or ^S – Control-PS – for underlining). Thus a piece of text may appear on the screen as

The use of ^Bbold^B and ^Sunderscore^S enhances your text

but not while it is still on the screen!

Other packages, realising the need to provide a display that is as close as possible to the final printed text, make use of the newer computers' abilities to display more than one typeface and the text will actually appear on screen as:

The use of **bold** and underlining enhances your text

This sort of facility has been termed WYSIWYG, another dreadful jargon term, meaning 'What you see is what you get'. Of course, this facility of showing the document as it will finally appear does not usually extend to features such as headers and footers.

Integration

The use of integrated packages, and other programs that allow you to prepare data in ASCII format, means that the results of other programs can be incorporated in your documents. A list of names and addresses from a database, a table of figures from a spreadsheet or the balance sheet from your accounts program, can all be included in the document, and once there can be manipulated like any other text.

Some integrated packages, such as Psion Xchange, allow you to move blocks of data from one program to another with surprising speed and flexibility.

The inclusion of blocks of graphics output is also extremely useful, as in the case of GEM Write, which lets you insert a GEM Paint picture between any two lines of text. This picture can be a drawing, graph or table of figures. The complete integration of text and graphics takes us onto the subject of desktop publishing.

Desktop publishing

It is inevitable that in the ever-changing world of the computer we are all constantly waiting expectantly for something new and exciting to come along. There was a brief period in the mid-1980s when it looked as if there were no great surprises left, but then Desktop Publishing burst upon the scene.

In fact, although it appeared to become fashionable very suddenly, it was more a case that it crept in almost unnoticed at first. The technology for desktop publishing was around for a long time before the programs actually began to become widely used. The evolution of more readily available enhanced graphics made the creation of desktop publishing documents on screen a practicality; the arrival a little later of laser printer technology made it feasible to produce the end-product in printed (and near-typeset) form.

The principle of desktop publishing is that you can combine text and graphics

by Inside Trader

CITY BEAT

A glance through any of the general business computing magazines, or through professional titles like The Publisher, will produce a crop of recent adverts from companies proclaiming, "We've been in desktop publishing since 1981/79/65" (delete dates as applicable). To which one reasonable and printable response is, "Balderdash". Nobody has been in desktop publishing for more than two years because, before that, it didn't exist.

It is only the latest generation of personal computers, microcomputer software, and computer printers which have allowed the development of true desktop publishing - the ability to produce, in words and pictures, publications which approach or equal the quality of the products of traditional typesetting and printing, and to put that power in the hands of ordinary individuals who have not been trained in the crafts of typesetting, page make-up and printing.

The desktop publisher may choose to employ a professional designer, or to have the pages output from a commercial typesetting system, or to use the services of a commercial printing company. But desktop publishing systems have given people that choice, a choice which was previously unavailable.

The increase in choice has been matched by a reduction in cost, so that this ability to produce high quality, printed documents is now available to many more people - individuals, amateur societies, non-commercial groups, educational bodies, small businesses and large corporations.

In the midst of the excitement generated by these recent developments some computer industry observers have noted that desktop publishing is a market doomed to die, and in a sense they are right. But only in the sense that desktop publishing will converge with other areas of personal computer use so that ultimately there will be one continuous spectrum of applications covering the generation and output of words and pictures, from simple word processing to complex typography; from quick sketches to full technical drawings and high-resolution scanned and digitised images; from simple page organisation to full graphic design; and from memo creators to book generators and all points in between.

The first stages of this convergence are already with us, and the would-be desktop publisher faces a bewildering array of software and hardware products. Some are wide-ranging in their potential applications, others are highly specialised. But the reader will find few of them in this book.

The reason for this cavalier treatment of these pioneering products is simply that they are pioneers. The manufacturers of software and computer hardware are constantly leap-frogging one another: in the Macintosh market the first page design package was MacPublisher. It was quickly followed and surpassed by ReadySetGo, which in turn was overtaken by Pagemaker. The latter program was long reckoned to be the outstanding leader in the field, but it was surpassed by version 3 of ReadySetGo in late 1986. As I write this in March 1987, a new version of Pagemaker is promised which may assume leadership once more.

In the area of IBM computers and their compatible competitors, the situation is even more confused. Although many products have been announced, few have actually made their way into the market. And what we have seen so far is merely the first step. Throughout 1987 there will be a torrent of new products as the industry matures, and the software developers receive feedback from the users of their early efforts. This next generation of programs will offer many improvements in power, flexibility, and in the ease with which they can be used.

(The intention of this book was to be non-specific as to hardware and software. However, I am a shameless devotee of the Macintosh. If the reader discerns hidden praise of Apple's brainchild, or implied criticism of other hardware systems, I apologise in advance.)
Serious discussion of individual products, then, is a worthless task since most of it would be out of date by the time this book finds its way into your hands.

Instead, this book attempts to address the subject of desktop publishing in more general terms: what it is, who can use the technology, why they might want to, and so on. You will find discussions of the different

16 High Roller: The magazine for the personal investor

Newsletter produced with a DTP package

DeskSet desktop publishing system from Altos

in a single document but with each part at any position. Unlike, for example, GEM Write, where the graphics can not have text to the left or right but only above and below, in desktop publishing the text can be made to flow around the document.

With most word processors you are limited to a single column of text; with desktop publishing you can have a number of columns on each page. Thus you are free to develop a newspaper format for your productions.

This new medium is being widely used for the production of newsletters, business stationery, sales literature and letters. It does have some disadvantages; the text is smooth and clear when produced by the laser printer but the graphics may still be the familiar pixel-based form, made up of tiny squares. This is sometimes a disappointment.

The text can either be created using the package, with all the usual editing facilities, or it can be imported from some other word-processing program. Similarly the graphics can be drawn within the package or be imported from a suitable graphics program. If you intend to use other programs in conjunction with the desktop publishing program, make sure that what you want to do is possible before you start.

Take care when producing documents for external consumption that the graphics do not spoil the overall appearance of the finished product:

- Straight vertical and horizontal lines will be perfectly reproduced, but lines at any other angle may have a step effect.

- Too much graphics makes the document look cluttered and the dotty effect makes it obvious that a computer has been used.

- Graphics images that are too small tend to be indistinct and poor representations of the real thing. A recent letter from an agricultural organisation had a heading that included a miniature tractor, leaving behind it four furrows that formed the border of the letter. A nice idea, except that the tractor looked more like a tap that had been left on with water pouring out, which was a little puzzling at first!

- There are generally fairly strict limitations on size. Usually A4 is the largest you can hope to cope with. However you should get a choice between *portrait* (tall and thin) and *landscape* (wide but short).

Desktop publishing first shot to fame on the Apple Macintosh and this machine is now often regarded as *the* desktop publishing machine. This fact has probably saved Apple from an early demise.

In fact you can get packages for most popular computers; in particular there are several very good programs for the IBM-compatibles. However, bear in mind that these programs tend to have high memory requirements (typically a minimum of 512K) and often only work satisfactorily on a hard disk machine. With all its exciting potential, desktop publishing is undoubtedly going to be the growth industry of the next few years.

Dictation machines

There will always be people who need to generate volumes of text, but do not have the necessary qualifications or time to enter it onto the word processor or typewriter fast enough for it to be cost-effective. As long as the entry of text depends upon the use of the traditional keyboard – and hence the fast entry of text depends upon special training and considerable experience – such people will rely upon others to do the typing and therefore need a fast means of passing their spoken words to them. Similarly, there are others who need to get ideas recorded quickly and permanently.

In all these cases one of the most obvious solutions is to use some form of dictation equipment. If you cannot speak directly to the computer and see your words appear then the next best thing is to talk to a cassette recorder and

Picocassette and Exec dictation system from Dictaphone

let someone else do the job of getting your words of wisdom onto the computer.

Of course, it is the principle of talking to a machine that many people cannot accept. It has to be said that walking around your office talking to yourself is not very impressive, and dictating while on the train will not only get you some funny looks, it will also acquaint everyone present of your innermost feelings on the given subject; the unfortunate typist may also complain of travel sickness arising from the constant train noises in the background!

These problems aside – and they are only minor ones that can be overcome by a little consideration of others – the use of dictation machines can considerably speed up the process of recording words and ideas. Having overcome the initial reluctance to talk to yourself and the horror of hearing your voice being played back for the first few times ('Is that really me?') you soon discover that your text can be permanently stored as quickly as you can say it.

It may take a while for your words to be unravelled again, with the inevitable long pauses while you are literally lost for words or the parts that have to be replayed a couple of times because of the dog barking in the background. In the end, though, the typed document will be a genuine transcript of your unbroken train of thought.

There are some disadvantages if you are working completely from scratch since rewinding the tape to find out what you have just said can considerably slow down the process. It is well worth preparing some notes before you start and at least getting the points in the right order. But don't forget that once it has been typed using a word processor or computer, you will have the opportunity to edit it extensively anyway.

As a general rule, dictation equipment consists of two separate machines:

- *A small hand-held recorder* This battery-operated machine records onto tiny cassette tapes and has a playback facility. Note that cassettes from one machine are unlikely to fit another, there being several different sizes in common use.

- *A desktop cassette player* This device will probably not have the option to record, though it should be able to wipe tapes clean. Usually it can be fitted with a headset to aid concentration on the tape.

The features you may expect to find on dictation equipment include:

- *Compact tapes* The small size of dictation cassette tapes and records make them easily transportable.

- *Headset attachment* This makes the typist's job easier as it cuts out disturbing background noise (except that on the tape of course).

- *Foot pedal* Inevitably the recording is at a different speed to the typing, so there is a lot of starting and stopping. Effecting this with a foot pedal makes life much easier.

- *Automatic backspace* Some machines automatically move the tape back a little way each time you restart, so you can hear the end of the part that has just been typed and the transition to the new text is smoother. The size of the backspace is usually adjustable.

- *Recording speed* Some manufacturers, e.g. Sanyo, offer a choice of two speeds for recording. The slower speed means you can get twice as much time on the tape, but there may be a reduction in quality.

- *Playback speed* Have you ever noticed that your voice is much deeper than you imagined when you hear it on tape? Well you can improve on this by varying the playback speed!

Philips have found that many users say that dictation equipment can save 25% of the time needed to get words into printed form, so there are clearly ways in which dictation equipment can improve efficiency throughout the office hierarchy.

All these features are attempts to come to terms with the fact that it is not as easy to 'see' a document when using a display screen. In this case the advancement of the mind is just as important as the advancement of technology. It comes down to the problem that the brain can accept at a glance a whole range of information from a single sheet of information far more easily than it can from the computer monitor screen. We have an amazing capacity to flick through a document of a hundred A4 pages, rapidly find the page we want and identify a piece of information by almost instantly building up a picture of the contents of the page. There is no need to read all the text; the shape of the document's contents is far more important. This is partly because we are trained from an early age in paper-handling rather than screen-handling, partly because paper is a more natural medium than the visual display unit.

Of course, there is no reason why this shape – in the form of paragraphs, headings, tabulation, bold type and italics – should not be transferred to the computerised version of the same piece of text. Indeed, it is probably the case that the text has been produced on computer and therefore the shape is inherent in the document. However, even the most advanced word processor is as yet incapable of producing on screen a faithful replica of the eventual printed page in a form that is still legible.

Most significantly, the 25 lines of the standard computer display screen can only show a portion of the page; even dedicated word processors with more display lines cannot hold an entire sheet for viewing. Inevitably some space is taken up with instructions and details such as current page number and document name. However, the 'shape', when in the form of varying typefaces, is more readily available on the better word processors and word-processing programs and this can provide some important pointers to the location of a particular piece of text.

Even with all the most advanced display features there is still the currently insoluble problem that the method of moving around a document, as with any other form of data, requires a mastery of the keyboard. It is second nature to manually flick through a printed document; performing the same task by pressing a combination of keys – whether it is PgUp, F6 or Control-C – requires practice.

Chapter 7

Handling data

The computer is fine for dealing with operations that we can manage ourselves if we have a mind to: typing, communications by telephone, keeping an appointments diary and so on. Where the computer really comes into its own is in dealing with large volumes of information: the company accounts, stock control, forward projections, payroll and many more applications.

Suppose you have a list of customers in alphabetical order but want to divide them into geographical areas or according to what they have purchased over the last year? Or you would like to get a really detailed breakdown of your accounts by department? Or you have produced a projection for the coming year but you want to know how this will be affected by a marginal increase in costs or prices?

In all these cases you can get the results by the usual manual methods but it is very time-consuming and costly if you have to pay someone else to do it for you. This chapter looks at those computer programs that can handle data in large quantities and with apparently effortless ease: databases, spreadsheets, accounts and stock control.

Database programs

Before considering any specialised applications it is worth looking at the generalised programs that store almost any set of data and convert it into meaningful formats.

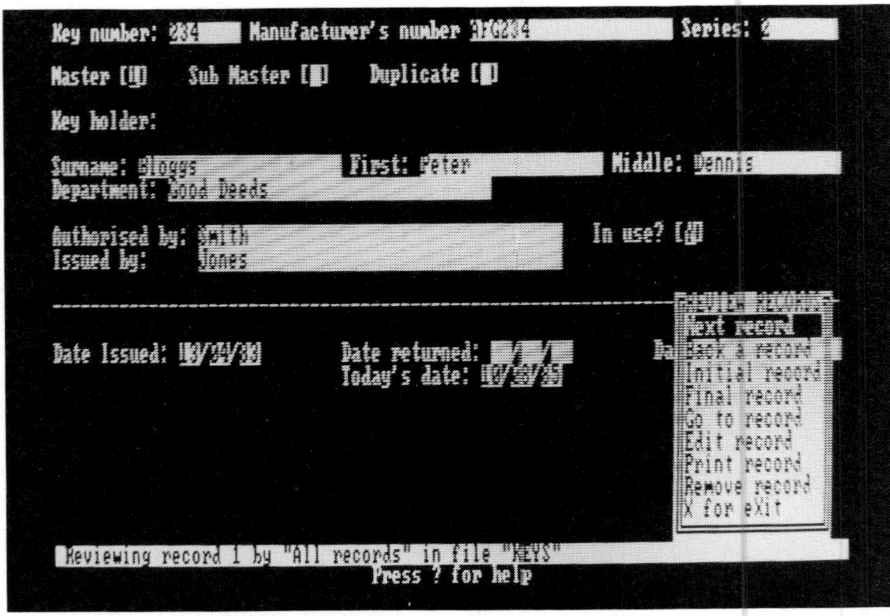

Data entry on a simple database screen

The collection of any set of data is usually referred to as a *database*. Most databases restrict you to data that is in a structured form. Any set of related data is stored in a *file* (in the same way as a single document or program is stored in a file). Each file is divided into *records*, the structure of each record being the same. Thus there may be one record for each customer or one for each product. Within each record you must specify the individual items of data, often called *fields*. So there is one field for the customer's name, one for the address (or one for each line of address) and so on.

The structure of files, records and fields is in fact applicable to most types of data and there are very few applications that cannot be fitted into this format, with a little imagination.

The number of fields per record may be limited. For example, Ashton-Tate's dBase II has a limit of 32 fields while dBase III allows up to 128 fields. Length of data in the field will also be restricted; the general limit is 80 but Caxton Software's Cardbox permits very long fields, up to 1024 characters (if you really feel this necessary; often fields of such great length indicate a flaw in the basic structure of the record and some re-thinking is necessary).

The ability to link one main record with a number of subsidiary ones, in order to link in additional files and supplementary information, is permitted by programs such as Comsoft's Delta-4.

The database program allows you to permanently store any information that is held in this structured way and then display or print it in a variety of formats. There are several different stages to using a database program:

- *Defining the file structure* This is an important stage, where you have to define the format of each record, including the type of each field (numeric, text, date, etc.) and its size. Some programs allow you to vary this structure later; in others the structure is fixed once data has actually been entered.

- *Entering data* The biggest chore is to actually enter the data onto the computer and edit out any errors. You can add new records at any time.

- *Producing output* The only point of storing information on a computer is so that you can get it back out again. A huge selection of methods is available, depending on the program, for manipulating the data. You may select records according to specific criteria and sort them into a different order before displaying them on the screen or printing them out. The printouts can be in many formats.

- *Combining files* The more sophisticated programs, such as the famous dBase II and dBase III, Psion Archive and many others, incorporate a small programming language that allows you to use your files in many different ways, combine files, produce complex printouts and perform many other tasks

Manipulating data

Perhaps the biggest problem with any form of information-handling system, whether a database, a collection of documents or the company accounts, is actually being able to find the item of information you actually want at the moment you want it and in a reasonable length of time. It is surprisingly easy to lose a piece of information; whether a single record in a database or a complete file of data. In the case of a record you may know roughly where a customer lives but if you cannot remember the name and this is the only field the program will allow you to use in the search then you're rather stuck.

Similarly, a whole host of records can be lost if you cannot remember the name you gave to the file, where you stored it on the hard disk or which floppy it was recorded on. In these circumstances, searching for a particular item of information can be rather like trying to find a particular book in the library when it is dark and you only have a small torch. Only a part of the data is visible at any one time so the process can be very frustrating.

To avoid this sort of problem you should be meticulous in the way in which you store information, in your naming and labelling techniques and in your approach to data storage in general. If necessary keep a written record of file names, disk directories and database structures. Then at least you can use some of the database features to speed up the search.

The features that you can expect to select from when choosing a database program include:

- *New records* Insertion of new records at any point in the file. Usually it is necessary to identify a *key* field (such as a reference number) to determine the standard order of records.
- *Field types* The cheaper programs only allow you to specify whether each field is to be text or numeric. Others provide a variety of field types, such as date, time, money, multi-line text, upper-case text, integers and real numbers.
- *Searching* Finding a particular record is eased by the ability to specify the contents of one or more fields and then display the records that match these values.
- *Selection* Similar to searching, you may want to select a specific group of records according to some criteria: for example, all customers in Devon or all invoices over £100.
- *Sorting* When you come to print records you may want to change the natural order. For instance, you may wish to print suppliers in alphabetical order of address or a collection of books according to publisher, with the books for each publisher being listed first by name of author and then in alphabetical order of title; later they can be re-arranged in order of ISBN number. The better programs allow several levels of sorting, sorting on any fields (rather than just pre-defined key fields) and re-sorting at any time.
- *List format* You should be able to choose which fields are to be printed and the order. You may print the file as a columnar list or with each record on a separate page or in a format that covers several lines.
- *Export facilities* The opportunity to put the selected and sorted data into a format that can be exported to some other program, such as a spreadsheet or word processor, is an added advantage.

These are only some of the many facilities provided by database programs. The flexibility of the program is best measured by a study of its in-built programming language. There is, of course, a price to pay for the immense flexibility of programs such as dBase III; that is you must invest a considerable abount of time and effort in learning how to use the program and the complexities of its language. If much of your time is spent on handling data this can be well worthwhile and very rewarding. However, you should not underestimate the problems that will arise when you start to take this level of interest in the database program. These are discussed in more detail in the section on programming in Chapter 5.

Spreadsheets

The need to carry out calculations on tables of figures and set out the results in a tidy and legible way is a large part of most businesses's operations. This category of work includes the preparation of projections and budgets, price lists, depreciation tables, interest tables and other similar tabular work.

All this work can be computerised and the most common method of doing so is through the *spreadsheet*. A spreadsheet consists of a rectangular grid of rows and columns; the intersection of each row and column is called a *cell* and each of these can take a single number or item of text. The normal convention is for columns to be labelled A, B, C, etc., while the rows are numbered from 1. So the contents of the cell in the fifth column and third row could be referred to as E3.

The great advantage of the spreadsheet is its ability to automatically carry out calculations and update the results when changes are made to the data. For example you may have three columns for an order list, containing product name (column A), quantity (column B) and price (column C). A fourth column may calculate the total value for each item. If the first row of actual data is in row 5 then the value is generally calculated by entering a formula in cell D5 in the form:

B5 * C5

('*' is used to represent mutiplication.)

As soon as this formula has been entered the result of the calculation is placed in the cell. This formula can then be automatically repeated all the way down the list. Another calculation can sum the contents of the value column to produce a grand total. The exciting part comes when you change one of the values or prices and all the calculations are automatically done anew.

Some of the more advanced spreadsheets (such as Psion Abacus) allow you to use label names from the tops of columns or ends of rows in the formula. So the value may be calculated by a formula such as:

VALUE = PRICE * QTY

This adds an element of friendliness to the proceedings and helps make the sheet more understandable. Of course, explanatory text can also be placed on the spreadsheet to help understand what is going on.

Spreadsheet facilities

Spreadsheets are as variable in the facilities they provide as any other software package. Some of the features you should look out for include:

- *Size* Many spreadsheets are very limited in total grid size (say, 26 columns by 100 rows); others can extend to ridiculous limits in both directions (such as 255 columns, 999 rows). This is all very well but before rejecting a spreadsheet on the grounds of size think carefully about how large the sheets you use really will be. Remember that large sheets are not only going to be difficult to handle on screen, they will have to be printed out in a number of sections. If considering very large sheets you should consider ways in which they can be broken up into individual sections on the sheet, with the results from each section being combined in a summary page.

- *Use of labels* Using text labels in your formulae is helpful but certainly not essential.

- *Automatic recalculation* Does the sheet automatically recalculate every time you make an entry or do you have to select a certain command to achieve this? If it is automatic, can you turn this feature off? (For large sheets where you want to make a number of changes, the lengthy recalculation times can make the process very tedious if this is not an option that can be turned off.)

- *Insertion and deletion of rows and columns* It is essential to be able to insert a new row when you discover that your projection contains no figure for May or you forgot an expense heading.

- *Re-ordering rows and columns* You may need to swap two rows or columns or change the order completely. One alternative is to use the block options which, in a similar way to those of word processors, allow you to move, copy or delete any block of data. Some programs allow rows or columns to be re-ordered according to the contents of a specified row or column.

- *Column width* Different columns will need to be of different widths, depending upon their contents.

- *Transposition* Turning the sheet on its side, by swapping rows and columns, is not widely used nor widely available, but is nevertheless sometimes a useful addition.

- *Units* It is important to be able to specify that a block of cells should have a fixed number of decimal places, be rounded to the nearest integer, etc. Sometimes you are able to specify monetary formats, the use of brackets for negative numbers or the inclusion of monetary symbols.

- *Justification* Text in any block may be placed on the left or right of the cell or centred. Better spreadsheets allow items of text to spill over into empty neighbouring cells if they are too long to fit into their original cell.

- *Print formats* The ability to print part or all of the sheet is obviously essential, but it may also be useful to print a list of the formulae used in the calculations. Psion Abacus is one example of a spreadsheet that includes this facility

Before choosing the package, you need to decide how the spreadsheet is going to fit in with the rest of the system. The spreadsheet is rarely the main reason for buying a computer so its compatibility with other parts of the

PR CE LIST

Order Code	Description	Price per Box 1-3	3-5	5+
001	Unbranded ss/dd	6.50	6.25	5.99
002	Unbranded dd/dd	8.50	8.25	7.99
003	Unbranded dd/qd	9.50	9.25	8.99
004	Datadisk ss/dd	7.95	7.75	7.50
005	Datadisk dd/dd	9.25	9.00	8.75
006	Datadisk dd/qd	11.75	11.50	11.25
007	Truedisk ss/dd	7.90	7.70	7.40
008	Truedisk dd/dd	9.00	8.80	8.50
009	Truedisk dd/qd	11.25	10.95	10.70
010	SafetySave ss/dd	8.15	7.95	7.75
011	SafetySave dd/dd	9.15	8.95	8.75
012	SafetySave dd/qd	11.15	10.95	10.75

Inclusive of postage - just add VAT

Price list prepared with Lotus 1-2-3

system may be paramount. Can it exchange blocks of data with the word processor and database? Can tables from your accounts be imported into it and results passed back?

One of the most sophisticated and popular programs is Lotus 1-2-3, which includes features such as these. Some spreadsheets, such as SageSoft's Options, include modelling capabilities and risk analysis calculating a range of results based upon variations in the original data.

A final consideration should be given to the graphical representation of your data. Many spreadsheets now include a facility for displaying bar charts, line graphs and pie charts based upon spreadsheet data. In other cases you can export the data in a format that is suitable for a separate graphics program. Whatever options you choose you should aim to end up with a package that is easy to use and fits comfortably with the other operations of the computer.

Accounts programs

For businesses both large and small, book-keeping is a drain on their most valuable asset – time. Most small businesses in particular cannot afford to pay someone to do their accounts. Paying an accountants, though necessary to produce audited accounts acceptable to the Inland Revenue, becomes expensive when all book-keeping has to be handed over to them.

Yet the necessity of keeping accurate accounts for Income Tax and VAT purposes is one that cannot be neglected. Of course there are advantages; a well-kept set of accounts helps the busineessman to keep abreast of his financial situation, to plan for the future and ensure that projects and cash flow are being kept within budget.

Sadly the unproductive nature of accounting often means that the accounts of small businesses are rarely kept up to date, undermining their effectiveness as a financial monitor and relegating the businessman to the role of unpaid tax collector. The maintenance of VAT accounts is a particular chore; it brings no reward, provides no beneficial side-effects and yet tardiness incurs harsh penalties.

The production of budgets and projections, the control of bank accounts and the monitoring of individual elements of a business are all beneficial by-products of business accounts that are often lost through lack of time.

The accounts package is a special type of database program, pre-programmed to deal with a specific type of data and produce results in a particular format. There is no reason why the spreadsheet and database should not be combined

Sage accounting package

to do the accounts but with specialist programs available there is very little saving to be made by this approach.

Accounts programs, by their very nature, have very complicated data structures and it is therefore expecting too much to think that data from one package can be transferred effortlessly to another. Some data may be exported to other programs (such as spreadsheets and graphics packages), but importing data in any meaningful way is unlikely to be a practicality. Therefore careful choice of your accounts package is of vital importance. If possible get a demonstration version of the program to try before you make the final decision.

There is a wide selection of programs on the market, ranging from large, comprehensive packages that are equipped to deal with all the complexities of accounting for the largest of companies to smaller programs suited to the cash book accounting of the smallest business. The trick is to select the package that is within your price range and that achieves the level of accounting you really need without supplying expensive and over-complicated options that you can do without.

The emphasis at present certainly seems to be on the more expensive programs that favour the large business. Many accounts packages are well beyond the reach of the small business budget, few offer the simple facilities that a genuine 'small' business requires and many that do are generally difficult to master or require substantial knowledge of sophisticated accounting practices. On the other hand many of the cheaper programs do not offer the degree of analysis that is so important to the larger organisation.

Features of accounts programs

When considering accounts packages, there are a few things you should look for if the program is to be easy to use:

- *No complicated preparations* There will be some initial preparations to be made but, unless your accounts are particularly complex, these should not be too time-consuming. You may find that there are detailed structures of customers and suppliers to set up, complex code systems or other time-consuming preparatory work. Check before you buy a package whether these preparations are obligatory or can be by-passed if not required. Nominal and other ledgers can be set up but you should have to do this only if they are needed.

- *Pre-set order of events* In some cases all entry of data must be done in a pre-set order; in others any details can be entered at any time and in any sequence.

- *Single entry for all transactions* You should choose a system where each item need be entered once only. Once in the system the same piece of information is used to calculate all ledgers, to reconcile bank accounts, calculate VAT and produce comprehensive year-end accounts.

- *Correction of mistakes* Some packages insist on strict accounting practices with any wrong transaction being cancelled by an equal and opposite entry before the correct entry is made; on others almost any error can be rectified at any time.

- *Standing orders and direct debits* These may be updated automatically when they fall due. Reminders may also be given to enter details of bank charges.

- *Access to current balances* At any time you should be able to list the calculated balances in all bank and cash accounts.

- *Essential details carried over from one year to next* This once-a-year operation should be done automatically and with the least possible fuss, including year-end bank balances, unreconciled cheques and unpaid invoices.

- *Sensible defaults* The program should try to make life as easy as possible for you. For example, when entering cheque payments the cheque number may be automatically incremented with each transaction so that the actual cheque number need only be entered if it is different from that suggested.

It is unlikely that you will find a single program that satisfies all the criteria you set for it. However, you should be able to find something that comes reasonably close. Do not be pressurised by a single dealer; perhaps more so with accounts programs than any other form or software, the dealer is unlikely to stock a vast range of products and will naturally want to sell those he has in stock. A good dealer will have carefully picked the programs he sells, but this does not mean that they will necessarily suit your own particular circumstances.

Facilities provided by accounts programs

Apart from the entry of transactions and the production of standard reports your program may offer some or all of the following features:

- *Bank reconciliation* Whenever a bank statement arrives the better systems take you through all unreconciled items. You indicate whether or not each one is on the statement and the current balance is calculated. Any mistakes can be corrected immediately, so you can always be sure that your accounts are accurate.

- *VAT returns* The bane of all businesses is the monthly or quarterly VAT returns. This is perhaps the greatest joy of using a computerised system. There should be no further work to be done. All the information is already in the system and left quietly to itself for a few minutes the program should do all the calculations of inputs and outputs and produce the necessary information on a replica of the VAT form. All you have to do is transfer the figures onto the real form and – an agony no accounts program can mitigate – write the cheque. Check that special schemes such as the new VAT Cash Accounting Scheme launched in October 1987 are catered for. It is also important to satisfy yourself that the program has been evaluated by HM Customs & Excise to ensure that it satisfies their rules.

- *Nominal Ledgers* This part of the accounts program involves the automatic allocation of every transaction to different headings, providing lists of transactions by heading and totals for each period or year.

- *Year-end returns* At the end of the financial year the system should provide a comprehensive set of figures for auditing.

- *Profit and Loss Accounts* The summaries of individual sections of the program can be combined with other information, such as annual depreciation, to produce an estimate of profit/loss.

- *Credit notes, discounts and interest charges* It should be possible to enter details of these at any time, possibly with special procedures to be followed.

- *Detailed analysis* You may need the option to break each invoice, receipt or payment into its component parts, with separate ledger numbers and VAT rates.

Most programs are based on a modular system, with a basic program to which may be linked other additional modules. This ensures that the program contains the facilities that are needed, but with no unnecessary and unwanted trimmings. The program can be expanded to meet the growing needs of the business by extending it to include extra modules.

The modules available may include:

- *Sales Ledger* Separate ledgers can be created for individual customers, providing access to a complete history of transactions for each customer, with simplified entry of customer names (possibly using a Customer code). Credit limits can be set.

- *Purchase Ledger* This is similar to the Sales Ledger but providing details of suppliers.

- *Budgeting* This allows a budget to be set for each nominal account (or department) for each month of the year. Comparison of actual figures with the original budget can be made at any time.

- *Invoicing and Statements* These sections allow the fast preparation of invoices; there may be a standard format or you may be able to design your own invoice. Warnings should be given if a credit limit is being exceeded. Invoice details should be automatically included in all the main ledgers; no further entries need be made until payment is received. The Statements section should create statements at regular intervals for each individual customer, with aged debt analysis. Printing of address labels may also be available.

- *Payroll* The company payroll is as complex to computerise as it is to operate manually but it can be well worth the time and effort. You may have difficulty in finding a system that is flexible enough to suit your own individual needs but there are some reasonable programs on the market. Statutory Sick Pay should be catered for.

It should be possible to find a total system to match your needs but great care is needed in comparing the systems on offer. Do not assume that the one your dealer is most keen to sell is necessarily the best, but be guided by what he says.

When you have selected a possible system, take the relevant documentation to your accountant to see what he thinks of it. It will be a complete waste of money if he has to start again from scratch at the end of the year because the system does not fit in with his methods. If the system is acceptable, however, it will revolutionise your book-keeping and keep you up to date with the current financial situation.

Other data-handling programs

There are many other programs that are designed to work with specific types of database. One of the most common is the Stock Control package that controls levels of stock by constantly updating the stock file whenever stock is moved in or out, warning you when stocks are low and calculating total stock values.

Job Costing programs let you enter details of materials, costs per hour and requirements for a specific project; from the details given they provide an estimate for the job. As a general rule you should not become too reliant on such a system and always check its suggested estimates.

There are also many packages designed for 'vertical' markets; that is, programs that have been designed for a specific occupation or profession. For example, there are programs for builders, hotels, video shops, solicitors, garages and virtually any other sector of business you care to mention. Since

However, any vertical software should be looked at very carefully. Sometimes it is only an adaptation of other standard software with a few buzzwords thrown in to make it look different. In general, though, vertical software producers supply very good, reliable programs.

From the many hundreds of data-handling packages on the market it should therefore be possible to find a selection that will fit all your data processing needs.

Chapter 8

Copying the printed page

It is often said that power lies in information, especially if you alone hold that information. But these days it is communications that are the key to success, particularly in business.

The ability to transmit information to some distant destination is crucial to the success of most business operations. Whether it is information for branches of your company, for customers, suppliers or any other individual or organisation, the need for fast and effective communications is of paramount importance.

Many types of information need to be transmitted and your customers will often gauge your efficiency – and hence whether you are worth dealing with in the future – by how quickly you respond and in what manner.

This is the first of three chapters specifically devoted to communications using equipment other than microcomputers. In this chapter and the next we look at ways in which the printed page can be reproduced and distributed. In particular, two categories of machine are covered: photocopiers for duplicating sheets and facsimile machines for transmitting the printed page over the telephone network.

The need for copying the printed page

The reproduction of the printed page is an essential part of all businesses, regardless of size. From the very smallest corner shop to the largest multinational, everyone needs to copy a document at some time or other; in most businesses the copying of documents is as vital as making the tea.

Generally it is also done far more frequently and is considerably more expensive. For this reason it is essential to know that you have the right equipment and that you are using it in the most cost-effective way.

These two chapters concentrate on the facilities currently provided for copying, either in the form of direct reproduction – as with the traditional photocopier or offset machine – or for transmitting a copy of the document to some other location, a task performed by the increasingly popular *facsimile* (or *fax*) machine. Both categories of machine can cope with any type of document – text, graphic or photographic – whether produced by computer or more traditional means.

In many respects photocopiers and facsimile machines are the antithesis of the computer. Whereas the express aim of computers is to reduce paper in the office – or so we have always been told – the copier, by its very nature, multiplies paper. In addition, computers aim to provide information in digital form so that it can be manipulated and transferred to a variety of different media, changing endlessly and limitlessly along the way. Copiers, on the other hand, result in a static document, unchanged and unimproved by the process (with a few notable exceptions).

Therefore we need to consider exactly how these two apparently alien technologies will fit together. In fact, the two branches of office automation dovetail very well, the copier supplementing the capabilities of the computer and overcoming its shortcomings and vice versa. Essentially it comes down to a matter of convenience and common sense; in some instances it is practical to save text on disk and view it through your monitor screen, transmitting it to other users via a network; in other cases it is faster, cheaper and more convenient to simply duplicate a document for hand-delivery, delivery by post or rapid transfer by fax.

It will be a long time before board meetings can take place without the use of paper. The idea of directors receiving their agendas, minutes and other papers through their own personal work screen and then having access to them on individual flat screens during the meeting is becoming increasingly feasible; but it is still a very long way off, if only because it is a concept that we as individuals are not really ready to accept.

The other advantage of the copier is that it deals just as effortlessly with a mixture of text and diagrams as it does with straight text. The problems associated with mixing the two forms, described in Chapter 6, have little relevance to the world of the copier. Of course, the ability to handle graphics doesn't stop at diagrams and bar charts. Photographs can be copied in a far more satisfactory way than any computerised scanning equipment can manage and in some cases colour is now readily available, though at a price.

Although computer graphics is advancing in leaps and bounds, the result, when transferred to print, is often indistinct and marred by the familiar 'dotty' image of all pixel-based products. If you want to copy someone else's work and that work has not been produced on a computer, then if you wish to include large characters or pictures, the photocopier is often the only alternative.

Therefore, for all these reasons, there is still a very big place for the printed page in the office. Filing cabinets will be with us for some time to come and photocopiers and fax machines, far from becoming extinct, will no doubt continue to go from strength to strength.

Photocopiers

Most people know what a photocopier is and are fully aware of its ability to produce a near-perfect replica of any form of document, generally creating an image in black and white. Indeed, this is probably the office automation product with which most people – certainly those in business – feel comfortable and at home. If visiting a strange office and needing to make a copy of a document you are generally pointed in the direction of the photocopier and left to get on with it. The features of the traditional photocopier are now fairly standard, tried and trusted and, in the smaller machines at least, there are few surprises.

Although the technology of photocopiers is advancing, this is an area of office automation where the changes are not dramatic. Photocopiers have been around for many years and are an accepted part of most offices. They still perform basically the same tasks as they have always done – though with considerable improvements in speed and quality – but they are fitted with an increasing number of 'bells and whistles'.

These facts should not come as any great surprise. When the avowed intention of a machine is to make a precise duplicate of a single piece of paper, faithfully reproducing every line, mark and dot, then there would seem to be little scope for artistic interpretation or imaginative extras.

However, things are not quite that simple. Forever trying to bring something new onto the market and enliven interest in their products, photocopier manufacturers do manage to come up with an ever-increasing list of claims for their products.

At the simplest end of the scale is the single-sheet, plain paper copier. There is nothing sophisticated here, just a small machine that will sit happily on a desktop, looking perfectly at home. It has only a very few buttons and its operation is remarkably simple (for office automation products, that is).

Just lift the lid, slide the paper on top, close the lid and press the Copy button. A few seconds later a copy of the original will appear. On the cheaper machines, enhancements are few and far between. There are generally options to make the copy lighter or darker and to automatically print a number of copies of the same document, but that is often as far it goes.

At the other end of the scale are machines such as the Kodak Ektaprint 300 copier. This machine can produce double-sided copies at the rate of 100 per minute, with the final documents being automatically stapled together. In between there is a vast range of models offering a bewildering assortment of features in almost limitless combinations. When choosing a photocopier therefore it is essential to have a very clear idea of what you want to achieve before you even start to make the first phone calls.

Photocopier costs

For small businesses in particular, a cheap and cheerful system, used only occasionally for duplicating an invoice or copying a letter, is probably all that is necessary. Remember the first rule of buying any office automation product: don't be persuaded to buy a more expensive model with a few extra features unless you are absolutely certain that you really need them and that your use of them will genuinely be cost-effective. The salesmen and the glossy brochures may try to persuade you that you need the ability to do double-sided copies on A2 paper with automatic insertion of dividers and stapling of the final document – but that after all is their job. Your task as the person responsible for the automation budget is to ensure that the money is spent most effectively.

It is very easy to get carried away when you start looking at all the amazing claims in the magazines and brochures. Like everything else you should go into the negotiations with a very clear idea of what you want to achieve. You need to ask a few important questions: what are you aiming to do with the product? How will it be used? What are the essential requirements without which it cannot perform satisfactorily? What are the extras that it would be useful to have? What savings (if any) will the machine make?

The first task in choosing a photocopier is to decide what sort of throughput it is likely to deal with. First, the machine must be able to cope with the volume. It's no good getting a machine that is very quickly going to cause internal traffic jams in the office. Second, if leasing or hiring, the deal you work out will probably depend upon an estimate of your throughput per month; getting this wildly wrong may lead to an expensive commitment. If buying outright you will not want to have to upgrade the machine for some time to come.

Inevitably some pretty hard-headed calculations need to be made. Make sure

Infotec personal copier – the 9012

that you include all the elements of cost in your figures, especially if you are not really sure if you need the equipment.

If you decide to lease a machine then you do not need to worry about capital outlay. However, you should be absolutely sure about the components of the monthly fee that is agreed. Typically this takes the form of a basic monthly charge plus a certain price per copy. All machines are fitted with a counter so that the service engineer can measure the use of the machine and you will be billed accordingly. However, make sure that everything is included in the price before you agree. Items that may be added on as 'extras' include servicing, repairs, insurance and the cost of the powder or other materials used to make the copy. On top of this will be the cost of the paper itself.

If purchasing outright, the equipment will be treated as capital expenditure. In calculating the cost you need to account for such items as depreciation, interest payments on the capital, and the annual charge for any maintenance agreements. Added to this fixed sum is the cost per copy, in terms of paper, powder, etc.

Remember too that the life of your photocopier will be linked to the throughput. Photocopiers are generally written off over a five-year period, but may, of course, be traded in for a newer model.

Perhaps hardest to quantify is the cost of the electricity to run the machine. Though negligible in terms of price per copy remember that this machine will add to your electricity bill. The running costs are higher than those of most office automation equipment. If you only do a few copies, with the machine switched off in between, then the warm-up times involved will make the running costs per copy disproportionately high.

You can set against these costs the savings that will be made. Inevitably there will be many invisible savings (from having information at hand when needed) that are almost impossible to quantify, as well as some invisible costs.

Having worked out the cost you should remember that in most areas there are a number of businesses, from the local library to specialised office services premises, where you can get copying done for you. In many cases where the volume of copying is not vast it can be much more cost-effective to take the work out to an outside bureau than to do it yourself. Having to pay each time you do some copying, or being faced with a regular monthly bill, is also a very good way of regulating use of the service and ensuring that it is used only when absolutely necessary. The hardest part of the costing exercise is to estimate how much the machine will really be used. If you haven't had a photocopier before the chances are that you probably don't have a clue about the throughput and it is almost impossible to estimate. In such circumstances it is probably best to lease at first to get an idea of your real needs. If you do have a good idea of the figure then you should add little bit to allow for unexpected use and future expansion.

Control of photocopier usage

The great advantage of photocopiers is that they provide convenience. This can also be their gravest disadvantage. It becomes very easy and convenient to make a copy of something you would not have dreamed of copying before or when you might previously have shared a document. Thus the arrival of the office photocopier also heralds the appearance of a potentially massive problem of control of expenditure; abuse of the photocopier is second only to abuse of the telephone.

Inevitably, even with tight controls, the use of the photocopier begins to mushroom. Indeed, if it is not being used for purposes that were originally envisaged or for something that will improve the efficiency of the business, then it is probably being under-used and hence is not cost-effective.

If many people have access to the photocopier then it becomes harder to keep track of its use and you can soon begin to accumulate horrendous bills at the end of the month. This is one occasion where convenience has a price, and it can be a very high one.

Finding a new use for a computer is unlikely to add much to the running costs. Storing your appointments diary on disk, for example, and making it available to others through the network, has little or no impact on expenditure. On the other hand, photocopying your diary and distributing it in quantity each week is a very expensive option that most cost-conscious offices cannot afford.

Inevitably it is necessary to keep some form of check on the use of the machine, whether it is owned or leased. Writing down the number each time the machine is used is the simplest method; this is a bit of a chore and can sometimes be hard to enforce, but keeping a record in this way is itself often an incentive to efficient use of the system and a disincentive to 'illegal' use of the copier.

However, you should remember that the most efficient use of the machine is not to have it standing idle all day. Beware false economies! Producing another copy of a document on the daisywheel printer may seem to save on the photocopying bill, but the cost of the ribbon could well make this a more expensive alternative. Nor is it a particularly efficient use of anybody's time to be continually calculating relative costs in fractions of a penny for minor jobs

Choosing a photocopier

Having settled in your mind a rough idea of the volume the machine must deal with, the next task, before you approach the dealer, is to decide what features you need and what would be pleasant accessories.

Make a list – preferably a short one – of the features that are considered indispensable. Above all else, talk to the people who need to use the equipment and find out exactly what their requirements are. This is probably best achieved by determining what tasks they want to complete and working backwards to decide what features would fulfill the requirements. This approach is generally better than asking what features they would like to see. Human nature being what it is, it is natural to desire facilities that are really only the icing on the cake. It is easy to be persuaded that four-tone colour is essential, only to discover that the facility is used just once a month and then only to enhance the office newsletter.

Some people will undoubtedly be avid followers of the latest developments in the field and will be able to think of all sorts of exotic uses for the newest equipment, but don't allow yourself to be brainwashed into anything that cannot ultimately be justified. If you don't understand a particular feature then make it your job to find out about it. Often the most persuasive and effective salesmen are the people in your own office!

It is here that it is essential to strike a balance. Do not write off any new ideas just because you didn't think about them or know about them. They are certainly worth looking into. In the ever-changing world of office automation it is important to remember that most people are probably at least as ignorant of the subject as yourself. Never be afraid to ask.

Having settled the list of features that are needed you next need to decide which of these can be dealt with most efficiently by going to outside services. Why pay extra for an A3 copier if 99% of your work is printed on A4? For the few A3 sheets that you do need it could well be cheaper to send the work outside. And remember that there are usually cheaper ways of getting the same effect. For example, an A3 sheet can be photocopied in two halves. Not very satisfactory for external distribution, but for internal use this is often good enough.

It may also be worth considering having more than one copier if the equipment is to serve more than one office: a large central one, with one person in charge, and other, smaller machines throughout the building for less demanding work.

Photocopier features

Most manufacturers offer a glittering array of features. Sifting through the specifications need not be time-consuming if you know what you want before you start looking. These are some of the most commonly available features from which you will have to choose:

- *Speed* Low-volume copiers produce in the order of 30 copies per minute (much longer of course if they are copies of different documents). High-volume copiers may make in excess of 100 copies per minute. One factor in determining the speed is the monthly throughput. Make sure that the throughput is not so great that a low-volume copier cannot physically cope with the volume.

  Also bear in mind that low-volume copiers are not really designed for constant, non-stop use. If your calculations indicate that the machine will never have a chance to keep up, you should definitely be looking further

The Selex 55 handles 15 copies per minute in sizes from A5 to A3

up the range. In particular, the high-volume copiers are far more rugged and able to withstand longer than a standard 8-hour day.

Another consideration is whether or not you are likely to need copies in a hurry. Do you have the time to wait while the machine chugs away or are you going to need a very fast turn-round?

Make sure that the promised speeds are genuinely attainable in normal use. It is frequently the case that the times quoted refer only to standard copying, without any of the special features being used. Some machines (such as those of Rank Xerox) maintain a standard 60 copies per minute regardless of what they are doing while others may drop to as little as a quarter of their advertised speed.

If the machine is to be switched off regularly after use it is worth remembering that some machines can take several minutes to warm up.

- *Paper size* Some machines will only copy pages of size A4 or smaller.

Many others will also supply A3 copying as standard. For larger sizes or other standards the choice is more limited.

- *Automatic feeding* Some of the larger copiers are fitted with the facility to automatically feed pages to be copied. This has the advantage that a stack of pages can be put onto the machine which can then be left to its own devices. Once again, whether this feature is needed depends upon usage. If most of the copying consists of just one or two sheets (or even the odd dozen pages) then the savings in time may not justify the additional cost. Alternatively, if you are regularly copying 80-page documents then automatic feeding is an essential attribute. Feeding of the blank paper into the machine is generally done through a removable cassette, but in some cases it must be fed manually.

- *Double-sided copying (duplexing)* This feature means that the copier can reproduce both sides of the sheet with only a single pass of the original. There is a great deal of wastage in trying to copy onto two sides using a single-sided copier. Having done one side of the copy you can guarantee that a few copies will be lost by the sheets being put in again the wrong way round. Other advantages of double-sided copying include a saving in paper, reduction in filing space and cheaper rates for documents to be sent through the post.

- *Colour* This is an expensive option that most businesses cannot afford. There is a wide range of options, from full-colour copying down to a selection of three or four colours. Colour enhances most documents, but it is often the case that a lack of colour is more noticeable than its inclusion. For example, a letter in black and white on black and white headed paper will stand out starkly and unattractively. If the letterhead is in colour the chances are you won't even notice.

- Reduction/enlargement Many copiers have the facility to reduce or enlarge a document. This may take the form of a few standard options, such as reduction from A3 to A4 or enlargement in the opposite direction. Or the copier may have a zoom option, in which the percentage increase or reduction in size can be specified in 1% increments. Some machines offer the facility to expand or reduce a document so that it fits perfectly onto an A4 sheet.

- *Collation* For the reproduction of lengthy documents in quantity the inclusion of collation techniques can be a tremendous time-saver. Here the machine makes multiple copies of the document and then collates them into separate stacks. The more expensive machines allow covers to be added, the automatic insertion of index cards and stapling of the finished document.

The control panel of the Canon NP-3525

- *Diagnostic panels* Most machines have some sort of panel to indicate when something has gone wrong. Photocopiers, being largely mechanical in their operation, are more prone to faults than most machines. In the more advanced photocopiers, these panels are able to indicate precisely what has gone wrong and many of the faults can be rapidly corrected by the user. The Agfa Gevaert X55-5 includes an instruction display that can be set to any one of ten languages.

- *Service agreements* Photocopiers do tend to go wrong, as noted above. Therefore an adequate service agreement with a reputable engineer or the original distributor is very necessary. Before taking on the agreement check to see whether or not it includes replacement parts.

- *British Safety Standards* Many imported machines do not comply with British standards, so it is worth checking on this aspect.

- *Machine size* The size of the machine itself may be a crucial factor. In a small office, a large cumbersome machine can make working unbearable. Portability may also be a factor. The Selex 55 is a desktop copier which produces sheets from A3 to A5 at a rate of 15 copies per minute.

- *Coin operation* For those really concerned to keep usage to a minimum a coin-operated copier may provide the answer! This is a useful option if you want to make the machine available to customers or members of the public.

- *Programmability* At the top end of the scale the machines can be programmed to automatically perform a complex series of instructions.

- *Processing type* Most photocopiers operate by thermal transfer. Some use photographic processing and it is these that can provide full colour and copy onto photographic paper or transparency film. This last case is ideal for the preparation of material for overhead projectors.

- *Editing* The most revolutionary changes have come in the introduction of editing facilities. An example of this type of machine is the Harris/3M 3060. This allows you to mark out any part of the original document for printing in a second colour. This marked area may be a diagram, an individual sentence or any other easily identifiable block.

  Any part of the document can be blanked out to remove unwanted marks or comments. Similarly, any section of the document can be reduced or enlarged. The quality of the copy is maintained so the new version can then be re-edited. This provides a tremendous amount of flexibility, but whether such advances will eventually be overtaken by new improvements in desktop publishing remains to be seen. In the meantime, they can provide some useful optional extras.

Additional equipment

Keeping tabs on expenditure is quite a headache, as described earlier. Therefore the addition of a control system may be helpful. This is an extra item of equipment that connects to the photocopier and logs the usage of the machine. It consists of a keyboard and screen that link to the copier. Users of the photocopier need to either enter a customer code or use a plastic identity card, or both.

The control system then logs all the copying that is done and links it to the relevant account. A printer lists details at any time or the information can be inspected on the screen. This is useful if photocopying is being done for customers who need to be separately billed, or for internal use to log the usage by individual departments for budgeting purposes. It also provides useful information when the time comes to upgrade the machine.

Some control systems will fit only specified copiers, others can be linked in to any copier.

Offset duplicators

For multiple copies the traditional offset machine has often been the answer. However, it has generally been regarded as too messy and complicated for it to warrant a place in the modern office. With the new generation of offset machines this is all changing.

Obviously these duplicators are not suitable for individual copies, but for long print runs the offset can provide an alternative that is both fast and cheap. Typically the cost of pages produced in this way is about half that of the same work done on a photocopier.

There can be distinct advantages to sending work out to an external print service, especially if the product is for internal use. An offset gives you complete control over the operation, so that you are fully and solely responsible for the final quality (which is not to say that you will be able to reach the quality achieved by professional printers). There are no long delivery times and you can specify precisely the quantity you need (though you should always allow some leeway for spoilt sheets and overall shortfalls). Price will also be an important factor. In some cases the offset can be linked to the photocopier, which is used to produce the plates from which the offset produces its copies.

Features you may expect to find on an offset include:

- *Speed* Typical speeds are 120 sheets per minute (often quoted in terms of 7200/hour).
- *Queueing* An offset may be able to work automatically through a stack of up to 50 plates.
- *Repeat counting for multi-page originals* If working through a stack of plates the machine may count the same number of printed copies in each case.
- *Alternate stacking* With multi-page originals each stack of printed paper may be placed in a different direction to ease the task of splitting the sections for collation.
- *Detection of misfeeds* Photoelectric cells are sometimes used to detect and adjust for misfeeds.
- *Automatic cleaning and inking* The feature that has made the modern offset an acceptable item in to-day's offices is its automatic facilities for cleaning and inking the 'blanket'. Thus you can happily spend an afternoon with the offset without getting up to your elbows in ink!

Optical character recognition

Computers are used to generate text. This can be reproduced through the photocopier and then transmitted, as the printed word, to some far off destination using fax or telex. To complete the circle, and provide the means to translate the written word into a form that the computer can understand, without rekeying it, you may use an optical character reader. This is a device that will scan certain typefaces and convert what it sees into a text format that the computer can understand. As yet, the range of such machines is still somewhat limited. Also in this category of reader are machines such as bar code readers.

Chapter 9

Transmitting the printed page

The evolution of modern telex and facsimile machines represents a major step forward in communications. A photocopier is fine for making a duplicate of a document for personal use, for hand delivery or for sending by post where speed is not essential. A modem provides the means to transmit computer data around the world in seconds. But suppose you want to despatch a document to the other end of the country and need it to arrive in minutes?

The answer to this problem lies in telex and facsimile machines. There are some important differences between the two classes of machine and although the fax machine can perform all the tasks of the telex, there are nevertheless many situations where telex is a more suitable option.

This chapter looks at the growing fascination with the communication of printed information across the telephone network.

Telex

Telex has been in use in Britain for over 50 years, yet it still has an important role to play. Telex equipment these days is very compact, resembling a small portable typewriter. Telex is a messaging service not unlike similar computer facilities (see Chapter 10), but with the advantage of having over two million established users worldwide.

3M Whisper telex

Features you may find on modern telex machines include:

- Built-in screen to prepare and edit messages.
- Memory for storing messages (often up to 32K).
- Routing of messages to several destinations.
- Communication with other devices.

Transtel Comwriter III – a screen-based telex terminal

Undoubtedly the full linking of the telex with other communications devices is the next logical step and will lead to greatly enhanced facilities.

Facsimile machines

While telex machines are well-suited to the rapid transfer of text across the telephone lines and modems provide the additional facility to transfer computer graphics, both these modes of operation come unstuck when we need to send pictures, diagrams, photographs or anything else with any form of non-standard output. This gap is filled by the *facsimile* machine, commonly known as *fax*.

A fax machine, defined at its simplest level, is a photocopier with the ability to transmit the documents it copies down a standard telephone line. As with photocopiers, the range of features is extremely wide and the resultant quality and effectiveness equally variable. Unlike photocopiers, fax has not been around for very long and in its short life it has seen some major and drastic changes.

The procedure for operating the fax machine is very straightforward and the results appear quite remarkable when these machines are first used.

The first stage is to set up the fax machine in much the same way as you would a photocopier. Next you use the phone to make a connection to the destination. Once all this has been set up, the transfer is started at the push of a button. Finally, when the transfer has been completed, the line is disconnected.

Of course, there are some drawbacks to the use of fax. First and foremost, the proposed receiver of the document must himself have a fax machine. This is not as obvious as it sounds! Before investing in a fax machine – and they are certainly not cheap – you should think very carefully about who is to be the receiver of these documents. Are the people with whom you wish to communicate owners of fax machines that will be compatible with your own? If not, are they likely to invest in fax in the near future or can they be persuaded to do so?

As with all new communications technologies, the purchasers of the first few models in the field often feel they are out on their own in the wilderness. If few people have the device, then there seems little point in buying it yourself until others have done so. This 'wait and see' attitude has resulted in the premature demise of more than one technology. (Remember 8-track cartridges and video disks?)

Once a technology breaks through this initial barrier, though, its rise to fame can be sudden and dramatic. It seems that fax could well be on the verge of such a breakthrough. New standards in quality and compatibility have taken the devices to a stage where many businesses are now saying that there is no point waiting any longer and sales are starting to spiral upwards.

The other side of the coin is that the acquisition of a fax machine opens up a new world of communications to you and you can start receiving information from others with whom you deal who already have the equipment.

In many industries this sort of rapid transfer is now becoming an essential prerequisite to continuing success. When dealing with non-computerised, non-text information then frequently the only alternative is to send by post. But in many industries, in a world that is shrinking fast, it is becoming increasingly unsatisfactory for important information to be delayed for two or three days in the post. No matter how good the postal services may become in the future there will always be an uncertainty over arrival which can be completely eliminated by the use of fax.

Once again, many of the reservations over the costs aspect of photocopiers apply with equal force to facsimile. How frequently will it be used? Can the job be done by some other means? Will the installation of a machine lead to unnecessary and prolonged use?

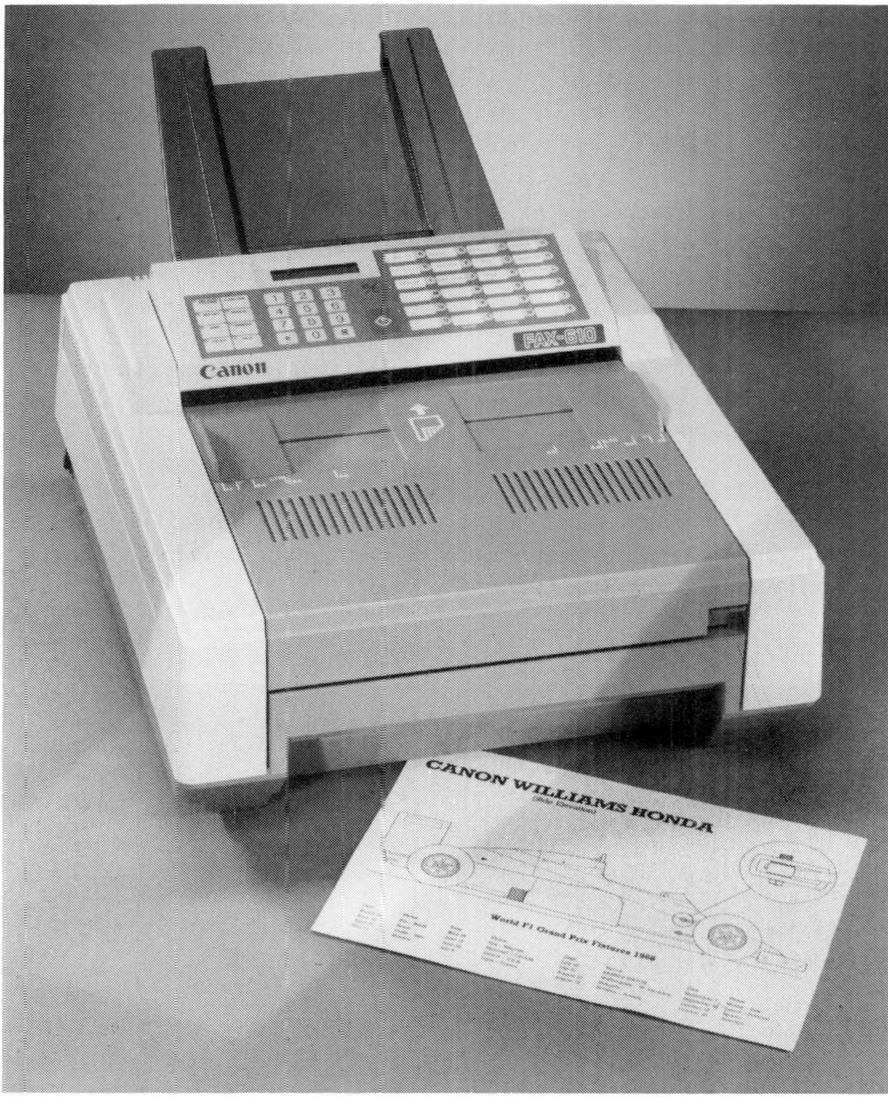

Canon Fax-610

These questions can all be answered by consulting with those who will operate the device. Again, the question to be asked is not 'Would you like a fax machine?' but 'If fax were installed, what operations would it perform and how would the results compare with what we already achieve without it?'

After exhaustive study of the costs of installation, with particular reference to the throughput of the machine, it may well be that you decide to use the fax services of a local bureau. For limited transmissions this is often the most cost-effective approach. If nothing else it can provide a good short-term solution while you assess the benefits of fax. It may also be that the bureau will offer you a service to receive fax messages as well as sending them. Their fax telephone number can be given to anyone with whom you need to communicate.

Most machines provide a test mode in which you can test the quality of the copy you will be sending by producing a copy on the machine. Although this does provide a form of copying as a side-effect it is not recommended for regular use and certainly not for producing large quantities of copies.

The facsimile document itself is often printed on special thermal paper, which does not give it a very attractive appearance. Fax is principally a method of communication, in the same way as telex, and not a means of producing polished documents. The paper is provided on a roll, which is guillotined after the appropriate length (but not necessarily a standard length). In a similar way to telex, fax messages are headed by details of the sender, typically the date and time, company name and fax phone number, and there is a page number for multi-page documents.

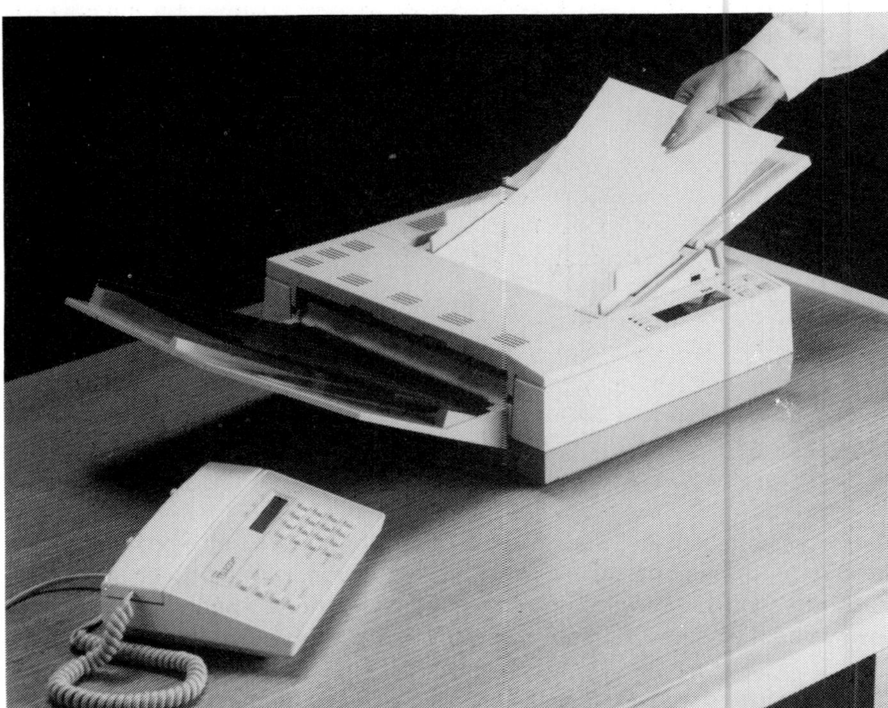

Rank Xerox portable Xerox 7010 desktop fax

Compatibility of fax machines

Before going any further it is worth considering the vexed question of compatibility. This arises time and time again with all types of office automation equipment, but it does not always relate to the same aspects of the machines. A fax machine is only any use if you can be sure that the majority of the people with whom you wish to communicate, not only have fax machines, but that they have machines with which yours can exchange information freely.

Fortunately, unlike computers, a number of standards were developed comparatively early in the evolution of the technology to ensure that different makes of fax machine could communicate without difficulty. Since the technology has been developing, machines have been classed in **Groups**, each Group having a set of specifications aimed at ensuring compatibility within that Group.

At present, three Groups have been extensively used and a fourth is coming into effect:

- *Group 1* This was the earliest form of fax, equivalent to the gramophone in comparison to to-day's stereo systems. These machines were extremely slow, the average time to transmit a document being of the order of six minutes, making the sending of fax an extremely expensive operation.

  They were also very unreliable, being highly dependent on the quality of the telephone link and easily upset by any noise on the line. Other disadvantages were that documents had to be wrapped around a drum in order to be scanned and the machines had a tendency to be rather smelly.

  This first standard originated as far back as 1968, pre-dating the main onslaught of the microcomputer revolution a full 10 years and establishing its pedigree as a non-digital technology.

  Group 1 machines are no longer sold and no doubt the original machines, though still occasionally used, will rapidly disappear as they are replaced by cheaper, modern machines.

- *Group 2* The second group of machines were an improvement on the first, but the technology was basically the same. The improvements instituted in Group 2 meant that the transmission time was cut in half. Although there was some improvement in performance, the quality of the line was still the deciding factor in the legibility of the final document.

- *Group 3* It is the introduction of the Group 3 machines that has really

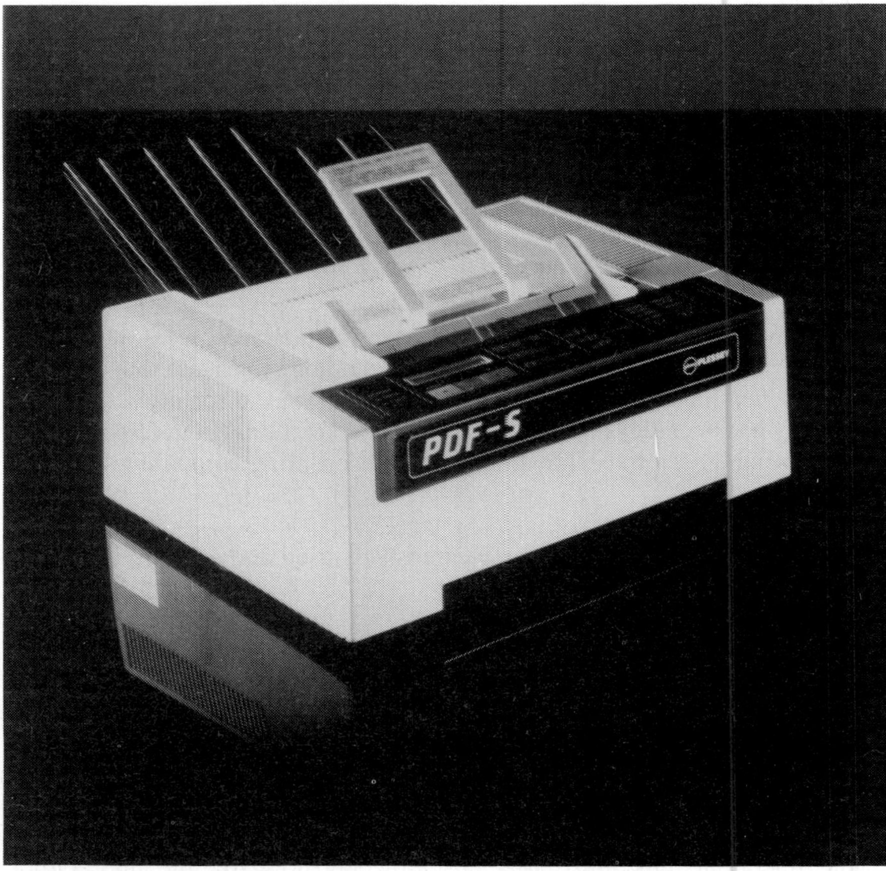

Plessey PDF-5 fax

put fax on the map and opened it up for all and sundry to use with ease. This Group has a completely new approach to the transfer of information. The document to be sent is converted into a digital form, bringing it into line with computer data techniques and matching it up with other new communications techniques.

The digital approach means that the state of the line is no longer a major factor in deciding the ultimate quality of the document when it arrives at its destination. It is possible to build into the machine techniques for checking that errors have not occurred during the transmission and, if they have, to retransmit the section of corrupt data. Procedures can be similar to those adopted by computers for data transfer.

Speed is now greatly improved, the typical transmission time being half a minute or less for an A4 sheet.

Compatibility should not be a problem. The standard was agreed in 1980 and has been generally adhered to so that you should be able to communicate with any other Group 3 machine. In general there should also be no difficulty in sending documents to and from Group 2 machines.

Of course, it is the digital nature of the Group's data that opens up whole new horizons for the future.

- *Group 4* This is the latest standard, based on the same techniques as Group 3 but with further enhancements. The documents are transmitted over special data lines, providing far higher quality and therefore open to greater speeds.

  Integration with computer networks becomes a very real possibility with these machines, as well as compatibility with telex. The arrival of computers and fax machines that can talk to each other with as much ease as their communications with their own kind is now tantalisingly close.

Fax features

The next major decision to be made, having settled the Group (the only real reason for selecting a Group 2 machine being the price), is which of the conflicting arrays of special features you consider to be indispensable. You are likely to be able to choose from the following:

- *Direct voice link* The ability to use the line for voice communications is often an essential feature. Unless you can afford to set aside one line specifically for fax, then it is going to be essential. Otherwise you might find that you pick up the phone only to hear the high pitched whistles of the fax transmission or people phoning your number are connected into the fax machine. The advantage of a separate line is that you do not have to be on hand to receive fax messages; the receipt of fax is automatic.

- *Speed* Some quite amazing speeds are now being advertised, but there is usually an 'overhead' that is not always mentioned. It can take quite a few seconds to make the fax link, identify the sender and so on. Once this has been completed the time to transmit a single page can be less than 20 seconds. This means that the total time for a single page can be quite large; for multi-page documents the average time can be significantly cut.

  It is worth bearing in mind that the speed of transmission between two machines is always dictated by slower machine. So there is little point in having a fast machine if everyone else with whom you communicate is plodding along at much slower speeds.

- *Portability* A number of small, portable machines are now available, notably the Sharp FO-200 and Xerox 7010. These are ideal for the salesman on the move for communicating complex orders back to the office.

- *Automatic feeding* For multi-page documents the ability to let the machine select the sheets automatically saves on transmission time and means that once the process has started the fax can be left to finish the task itself.

- *Delayed transmission* Many machines allow you to store documents which they then transmit at cheap rate times. This can, of course, result in considerable savings in costs. It is also dependent upon the fax machines at the documents' destinations being on their own separate lines and permanently connected.

- *High resolution and contrast control* Switches to improve or vary the quality can be crucial for documents containing detailed diagrams. Remember that digital Group 3 machines will produce documents constructed entirely from tiny blocks (similar to dot-matrix output) and there are therefore no perfect curves. However, the resolution is generally very high.

  Up to 16 shades of grey may be available but in most cases you are restricted to plain black and white.

- *Document size* The ability to send A3 documents can be a bonus, though to get the full effect the machines with which you communicate should also be able to cope with A3.

- *A3 reduction* If you are likely to be communicating with A3 machines but do not want the expense of A3 yourself, then the ability to automatically reduce such documents to A4 size can be a handy addition.

- *Compatibility* Not all Group 3 machines offer complete Group 2 compatibility, so be warned!

- *Display panel* Indication of who you are contacting, any errors that occur, and other similar information can be useful.

- *Permanent record* Many machines print a despatch slip whenever a fax is sent, giving details such as time and date, to whom the message was sent, and the time taken to send. This provides a permanent record of the transmission. A collation of all such details helps to control costs and to give an indication of potential usage when you are ready to upgrade the machine.

Canon Fax-910 plain-paper facsimile with advanced Group 3 features and output via a laser beam printer

- *Polling* This involves the machine that is to receive the document instructing the sender to start transmission, without any need for an operator to be on hand at the other end (assuming the document has already been loaded, of course). For example, the NEC Nefax-18 has the ability to poll up to 60 locations. So each of your branches can prepare a regular report and this can then be automatically despatched on instruction from head office.

- *Automatic re-transfer* You may require the ability to redistribute a fax, as soon as it is received, to other locations.

- *Copy mode* Using the fax as a copier is sometimes handy, but this mode is generally used to test the quality of the transmission. This is particularly important if you are sending highly detailed work, since much of the detail can be lost when the digital version is produced.

- *Plain paper* If you are not keen on the special fax paper, an increasing number of machines work with plain paper. These work on either a a thermal transfer process (for example, the Canon Fax-610) or, more expensively but with higher quality, using a laser beam printer (such as the Canon Fax-L910).

- *Telephone features* Features found on most telephone systems, such as automatic redial and stored directories are often included.

- *Security* If security of information is a worry to you then you may consider the need for users to enter a Personal Identity Number (PIN) in order to gain access. Alternatively encryption units will code the data at the sender's end and decode it at the receiver's. Both these options are offered by the ITT 3536, marketed by Fulton Communications.

Computer communications

Perhaps the most exciting prospects for the future lie in the options that are becoming available to link into other 'traditional' office automation equipment. The digital nature of Group 3 and Group 4 machines opens up the whole world of computer communications.

It is now possible to transmit documents direct to a computer fitted with a modem. The document that is received can of course be edited and adapted in the same way as any other product of computer graphics. In a similar way it is feasible for a computer to despatch its files directly to a fax machine.

Other possibilities lie in the ability to connect the fax machine to an optical disk, providing permanent storage of millions of documents. This end of the new technology is still in its early stages, but it represents another important link between separate elements of the office automation world.

This convergence work is being pioneered by Pitney Bowes with their 'Path' system. Software allows a specially programmed fax to communicate with a suitably equipped IBM or IBM-compatible. Undoubtedly this is going to provide the basis for the next giant step forward in fax technology and we can hope to see extremely advanced communications devices, able to talk to all manner of digital equipment, arriving in our offices over the next few years.

Chapter 10

The telephone network and communications

The most widely used and indispensable item of office automation equipment must surely be the telephone, in all its various guises. The network to which it is connected provides the basis for communication channels that can support many different types of transmission, though all based on the same principles and technologies. The telephone network currently has a number of distinct uses:

- Voice links between individuals for normal communication.
- A link between two fascimile machines for transmitting documents.
- Messaging facilities for electronic mail.
- Access to databases and similar services.

Although these services are still fairly distinct there is no doubt that as the technologies converge it will become harder to tell the difference. It is no longer an impossible dream to imagine information from some distant database being incorporated into a computer document that is then transmitted to some other location, there to be printed out on a waiting fax machine, perhaps even with a voice message attached.

This chapter looks at the telephone equipment that inhabits all of our offices and is indispensable to most business operations and other organisations, as well as playing a vital role in the lives of most individuals.

Telephones

Gone are the days when a 'telephone' was a black box with a handset on the top and a ten-digit dial on the front. Nowadays telephones are supplied with a range of extra buttons, displays and memories. The number of manufacturers is increasing now that the equipment that can be plugged into the network is no longer limited to British Telecom's own brand. However, don't forget that anything you connect into the national network must be marked with BT's green 'Approved' symbol.

Some of the features you may find on standalone telephones include:

- LCD display to show the number you are dialling or have just dialled.
- Automatic redial of the last number (or one of the last ten).
- Secrecy button so that you can talk in confidence to the person in the office who is 'not in at the moment'!
- Memory of anything between 10 and 250 numbers. These are selected by pressing a memory key or (in the case of BT's QWERTYphone with a massive choice of telephone numbers) a sequence of letters.

QWERTYphone from British Telecom

Northern Telecom Displayphone, which permits voice and data communications to be handled in one unit

- Current time and date.

- Call timer to tell you how long you have spent on any call. In some cases you can type in the current charge bands and rates, and this information, linked to the time and date, will tell you how much the call actually cost. A frightening process, but excellent for keeping the bills down!

- Conference facilities, where several extensions can be linked into a single call so that all users can communicate with each other as if sitting in the same room.

Switchboards

For most businesses, one telephone line is insufficient and a number of lines must be controlled, leading to a system with a number of extensions. The range of equipment needed to cope with the complexities of the office telephone system is vast and needs to be tailored to suit the needs of each organisation. No two businesses are the same and, as a result, very few businesses have exactly identical internal telephone systems. If the precise

Some BT telephone systems

combination of equipment you require is not immediately obvious to you, the services of a reliable and well-qualified telecommunications consultant can be of immense help; such services easily pay for themselves by saving you from investing capital in – or leasing – expensive equipment you do not need.

Basically, there is a choice between a Key and Lamp, a system with a switchboard operator, or the Private Automatic Branch Exchange (PABX).

The key and lamp system shows the status of each line, whether it is free, busy or on hold. The system allows you to link incoming calls with specific extensions. It may be linked into your PABX.

Modern systems, such as Norton Telecommunication's Multiline key and lamp system, are easy to use and provide far more information than their original ancestors. The Multiline gives information such as the call that is at the front of the queue as well as the ability to link any call with any extension. Some systems also include intercoms and can be connected to call-logging equipment.

Other manufacturers of key and lamp systems are Telephone Rental, with

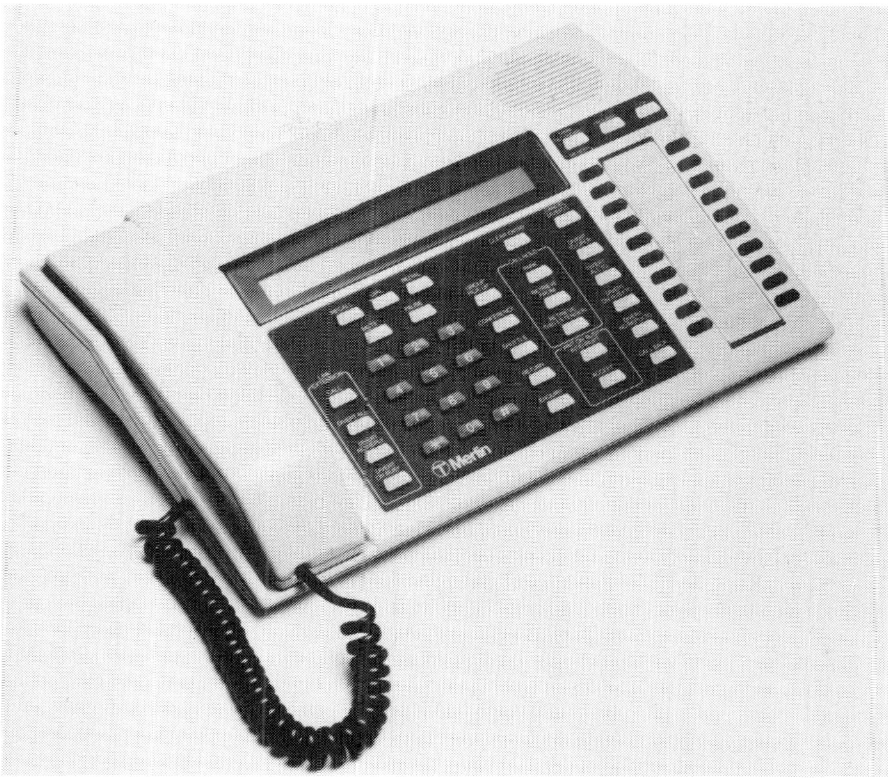

BT Merlin TX72 featurephone

their TR1232 system (catering for 12 lines and 32 extensions) and the Merlin Septara (16 lines and 48 extensions) from BT Business Systems. The Philips Sopha S system is also becoming widely used.

Ferranti, Norton, Plessey and Telephone Rentals are amongst the leading PABX manufacturers. BT's IT440 combines voice and data transmissions in a single, integrated network.

Cellular phones

Cellular radio is a rapidly expanding sector of the telecommunications market. These radio telephones allow you to keep in contact with others while on the move. Each phone is in radio contact with a small local transmitter. This in turn is part of a much larger, national network. As you move from one area to another the computer that controls the system ensures that the link is made smoothly so that you do not notice the transition.

Racal Citifone – a compact cellular telephone

Main contenders at present are BT's Cellnet and Racal/Vodafone and both are expanding their areas of coverage.

Features you might find include:

- Automatic redialing of last used numbers.
- A hands-free facility.

One-to-One goes in-car: a cellular telephone link for electronic mail users

- LCD display of current numbers.
- Diversion of calls to another number.
- Security options, to avoid unauthorised use or to restrict calls to pre-determined numbers.

Call logging

Telephones may be an essential component in any business, but they can also be very expensive to keep. For this reason alone, many companies invest in call-logging equipment. This comprises devices that are connected up to your telephone or PABX and monitor all calls that are made, recording the duration and destination of calls (and hence the costs) and providing a range of other details. This operation in itself can result in huge savings, not only because of the awareness of those who use the system that their calls are being logged, but also because of the indications the logger gives of how efficiently the telephones are being used.

However, reductions in bills are not the only reason for installing a logger. Other benefits include:

- Errors in telephone bills or faults in phone meters can be detected.

Telecost 64, a telephone management system that will monitor switchboards with up to 1600 lines

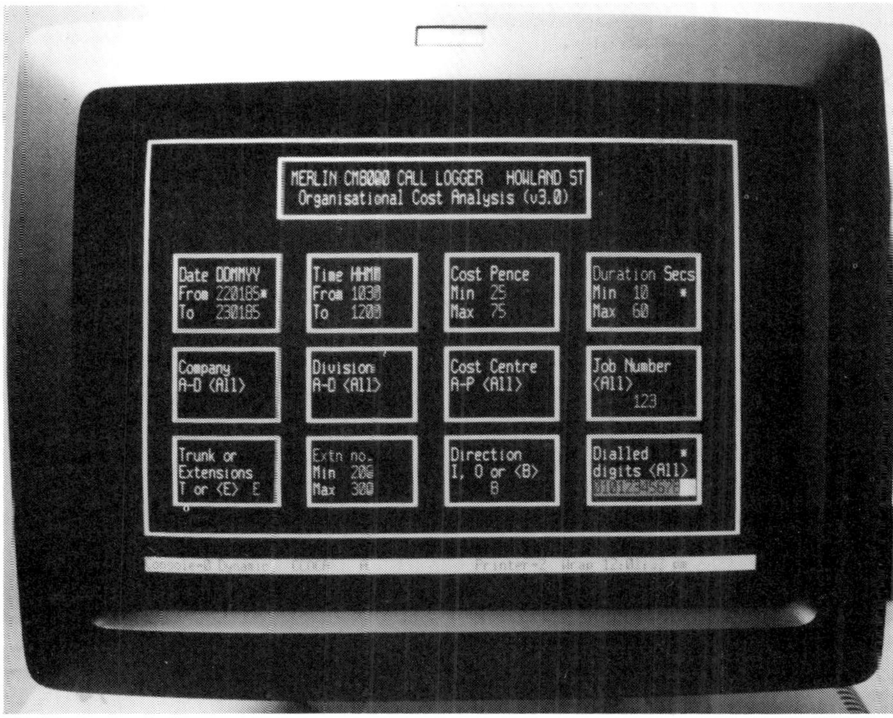

BT Merlin CM8000 call-logging screen

- The logger helps to ensure that phones are being used for the proper purposes.
- The results of the log can be divided between different departments, helping to allocate costs and plan budgets.
- It is easier to establish what modifications to the system as a whole are needed to reduce response times, eliminate many of the lost calls and lessen operator stress.
- If you are expanding the business or setting up a new department, the call logger helps to decide how many lines are needed and whether they all need to be two-way lines or some can be just for incoming calls.

Loggers operate in a number of different ways. For example, all the data may be stored on hard disk. Typically a hard disk will hold up to 18 months' data, as is the case with Automatic Switching Ltd's ASL 3011(S) logger.

Other systems are smaller and portable, such as the ASL 3064.

Radio paging

Radio paging has advanced as quickly as any other aspect of office automation in recent years. It is no longer the case that the bleeper you carry with you does just that: it bleeps and you are expected to rush to the nearest public telephone to find out what is the matter. For many professions this is just not feasible; public telephones tend to be few and far between if you are in the middle of Dartmoor or at the top of a building site.

Radio pagers are ideal for people who are away from the office for long periods, but some of the extra facilities now provided make these little machines far more useful than their simple predecessors. Therefore you can expect to find a range of other features from which you can choose the pager that really suits your needs:

- *Direct links to a PABX* The pager can be bleeped from any extension on the system.
- *LCD display* This can show a short message or code. How it is coded is up to you, but it is certainly useful to be able to indicate whether the bleep means 'Phone home when you've got a spare minute' or 'Help! The office is on fire!'.
- *Automatic paging* Pagers can be connected into the security system, for example, so that any intruder automatically triggers the bleeper.

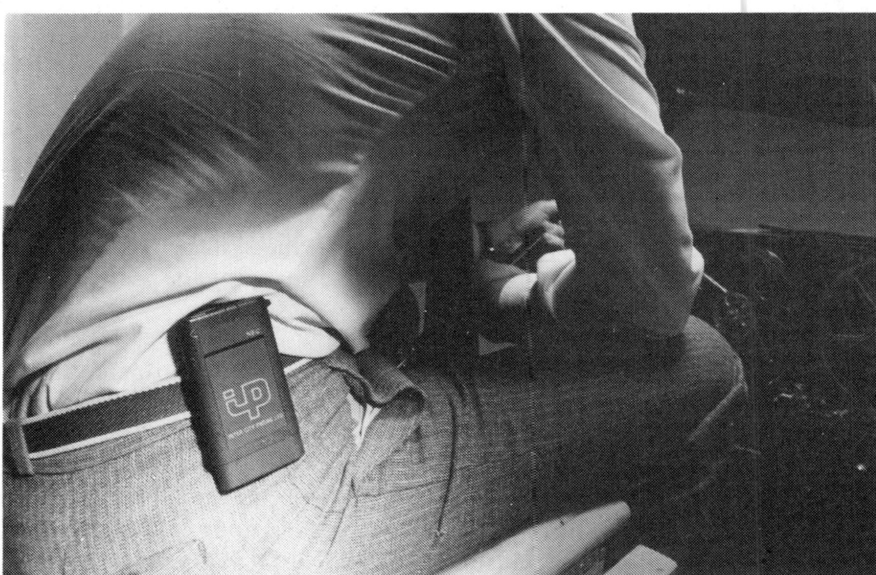

Inter-City Paging's 'Silent' pager

Multitone ICR 101 radiopaging/intercom system

- *Regular paging* Some systems automatically trigger the bleeper at predefined intervals. The person being bleeped must respond within a given time, otherwise an alarm is triggered. This is particularly useful for individuals working alone in dangerous situations.

- *Multiple paging* This is particularly useful for calling an emergency repair team, for example. With a single instruction the operator or automatic system can page the group of people most suited to the current crisis.

- *Voice contact* Some systems are more like small radio telephones, providing a link to the office or even a link between two pagers.

Answering machines

As mentioned earlier, one of the greatest disincentives to the use of dictation equipment is that people often feel foolish talking to a machine. Even worse than that is having to talk to somebody else's machine. This is no doubt the reason that many of the calls made to answering machines result in no message being left.

Despite a certain amount of public resistance, answering machines are, however, on the increase. It is certainly very useful to be able to set up the telephone to automatically take messages while you are out of the office,

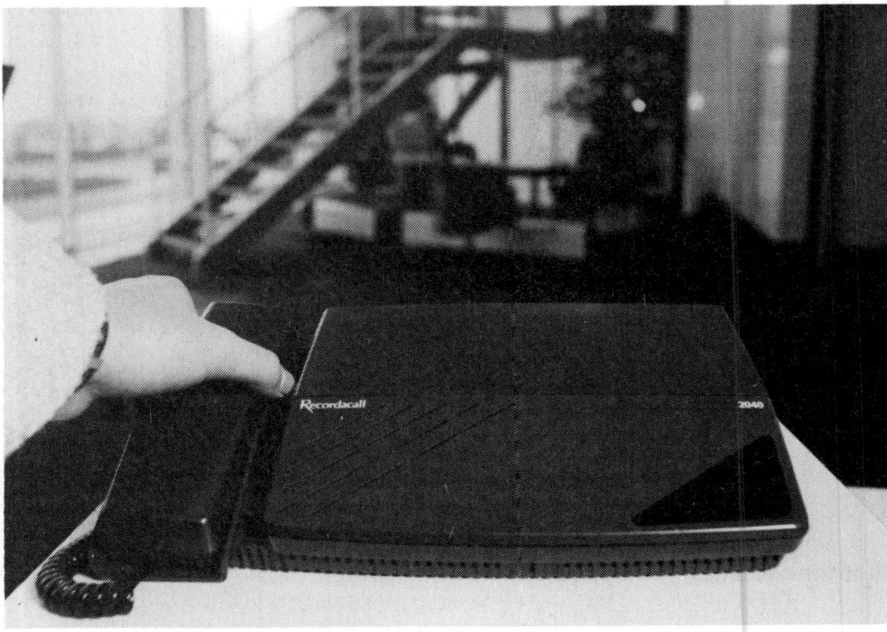

Recordacall 2040 telephone answering machine from Vanderhoff

especially if you have a job that takes you outside for a large proportion of the time or if you have friends who like to indulge in late-night telephone calls.

The most famous of the answering machines must surely be those produced by Ansafone, recently taken over by National Telephone Systems. Other manufacturers include Sanyo and Phillips. As with any other form of office automation equipment, there is a range of features, with prices to match.

Accessing the network by computer

The section on databases described searching for lost information as rather like looking for a book in a library using only a torch. Finding somebody else's information with a computer connected to the telephone network is like going outside with a torch in the dead of night. There is a great deal to see, but only a little is visible at any time, and you really do need to know where to look.

There is a great wealth of information now becoming increasingly available on other people's mainframe computers, much of it free of charge or accessible very cheaply. The main problem (having first decided what information you would like) is how to find this data and where to start looking.

Minimodem 3005 acoustic coupler

Miracle Technology WS4000 modem

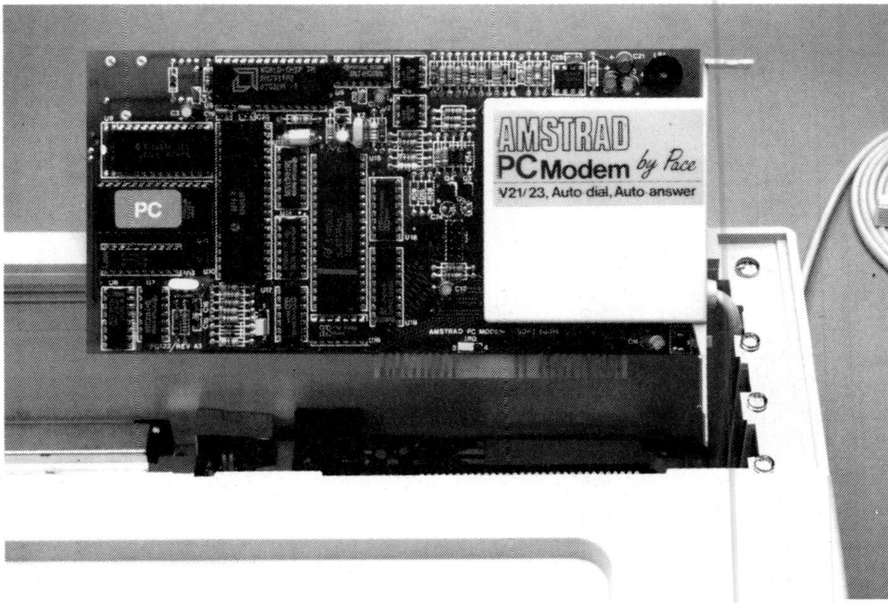

Pace internal modem for the Amstrad PC

Many distant databases are available for you to browse through. All that is needed is some suitable software and a modem, which is a device that translates data into a form that can be transmitted over the telephone network and vice versa. The modem plugs directly into a telephone socket. Generally, it is a separate piece of equipment, but in the case of the ICL One-per-Desk, for example, it is incorporated in the basic machine. Alternatively, you may use an acoustic coupler, a device that sits between the computer and the telephone, the telephone handset fitting into the coupler.

In order to make the most of the facilities provided by linking into the telephone network, you obviously also need a list of suitable telephone numbers. These are available through user groups, local computer groups and professional bodies. British Telecom will give details of its own particular services.

For many of the services described below the computer acts as a terminal. That is, it does not do any actual processing itself, but functions purely to send and receive information to and from a host computer, usually a mainframe. The computer at the other end of the link treats your computer as if it were its own keyboard and monitor.

In other cases the services use a system called Packet SwitchStream (PSS). Here there is no direct link between the two computers. The information from the first computer is transmitted in small sections, called packets. Each packet is headed by the 'address' of the second computer, which is a special code indicating its destination.

The packet is then sent to the nearest point on the network (rather like posting a letter in the nearest letter box). Once on the PSS network the packet is passed from one point to another until it reaches its destination.

PSS is used by services such as Prestel and Telecom Gold. Each user is allocated an individual PSS number that then provides access to many more computers. The great advantage of PSS is that the cost of sending a message is only that of getting it to the nearest point in the network and is not related to the distance travelled to its ultimate destination. Even very long-distance connections can therefore be made at cheap local rates.

Services supplied over the telephone in this way are grouped together under the heading Value Added Network (VAN) services.

SageSoft's Chitchat is a good all-round communications program that allows you to send and receive files to and from other computers or to access bulletin boards, electronic mail facilities and mainframe databases. It can be run on a variety of microcomputers which is an added bonus, since the transfer of data

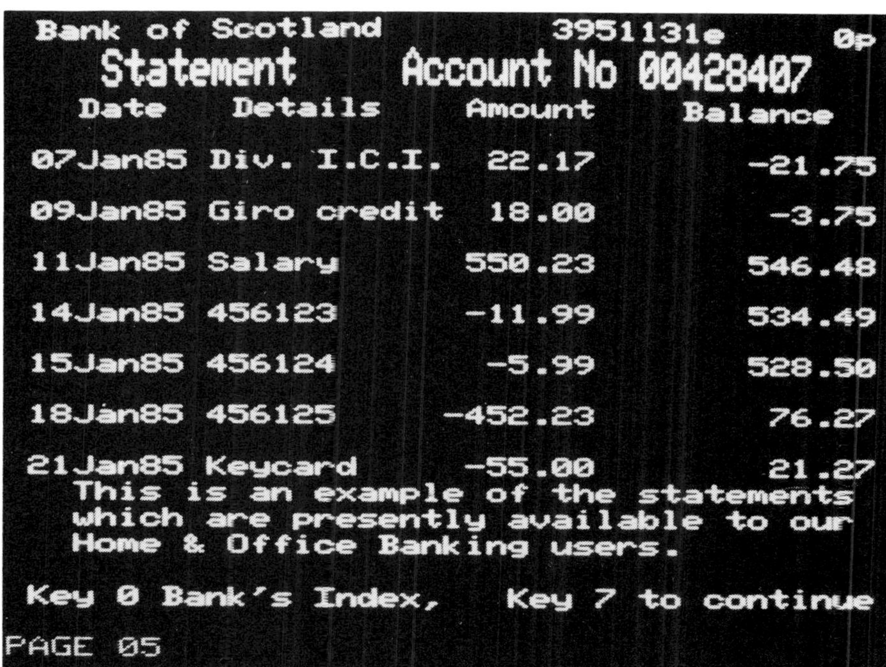

Home banking screen

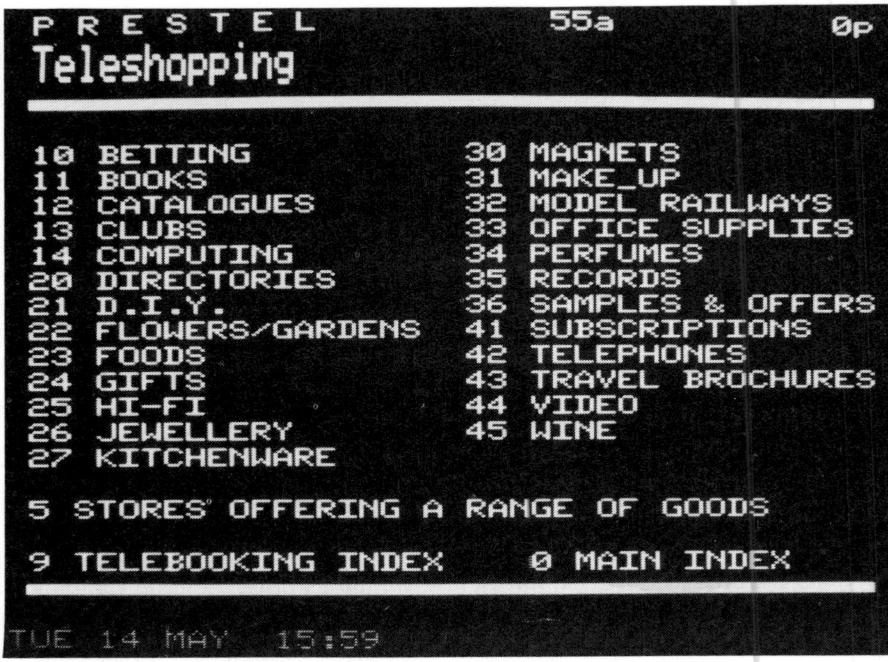

Home shopping screen

between micros is far easier if you have the two machines side-by-side running the same software.

The services you may access include:

- *Databases* These are large stores of information, often relating to a particular topic. For example, the British Library's Blaise-Line contains details of printed material, Eurolex provides data on taxation and law reports, Datastream International gives financial services, Dialog and Knowledge Index supply information on technical, scientific and commercial subjects. More general information is available from Prestel, described in greater detail below.

- *Electronic mail* The ability to transmit messages to other users is provided in a number of forms. Some links are fixed to specific computers (such as the Messaging facility of the OPD Tonto), while others are more general. Compuserve Information Services offers an international messaging service. Telecom Gold is a useful messaging service in the UK.

- *Office services* Some organisations provide services such as database, diary and word-processing facilities, in addition to the standard electronic mail.

- *Home banking/shopping* A number of shops, banks and building societies now provide facilities for ordering goods, checking your bank balance and so on, either via your own computer or through a special terminal that they supply. This is undoubtedly going to become a growth area in the future.

- *Bulletin boards* Although these do have some serious applications, they are also the 'fun' side of linking up with the outside world. They are essentially massive notice boards, stored on computer and generally available to all. Thus they may store messages for other users, advertisements, computer games, programs for general use and provide 'meeting points' for individuals sharing an interests.

There are two main ways in which all these services operate:

- *Glass teletype* Here the computer acts as a terminal and each separate part of the enquiry/response sequence starts a new line, with the display scrolling as the screen is filled (rather like the traditional operating system approach).

- *Viewdata* Sometimes called Teletext, this takes the form of the familiar chunky displays seen on television on teletext screens. The display is made up of a limited number of type-styles and a range of block graphics characters. The information is provided a page at a time rather than line by line.

In order to make use of any of these services you need a program that will set up the necessary link. Before you can gain access you may have to supply a few technical details such as the speed (baud rate) and details such as parity and number of stop bits.

You may also need to specify whether a line feed is to be automatically supplied at the end of each line of text (getting this wrong is not disastrous, it merely results in either an extra blank line being displayed between each line on the screen or each line overwriting the previous one). You do not need to know what all these terms mean. It is sufficient to know the values that are required and these should be readily available along with the telephone numbers.

Having entered these details (sometimes called the profile) and dialled the number, the connection should, hopefully, be made. In some cases a password is needed to complete the connection.

After that you are in the host system and free to browse amongst the data on offer. As a general rule you are given guidelines on how to conduct a search or help screens are available. In any event a little experience will show you how to get the best out of the system and how to find the information you want quickly and cheaply.

Communicating with mainframes

There are some fairly specialised programs that allow your microcomputer to emulate a mainframe terminal, i.e. act as if it is actually a piece of the mainframe hardware with no processing capabilities of its own. Some products let you transfer files directly between mainframe and micro. The product you need will depend upon the specific mainframe with which you wish to communicate.

British Telecom services

British Telecom provide several services that can lead to a multitude of independent databases. Browsing through these can be fascinating, but remember that it can become a very expensive hobby! On registering for Prestel you are given a local telephone number (where possible), so costs are

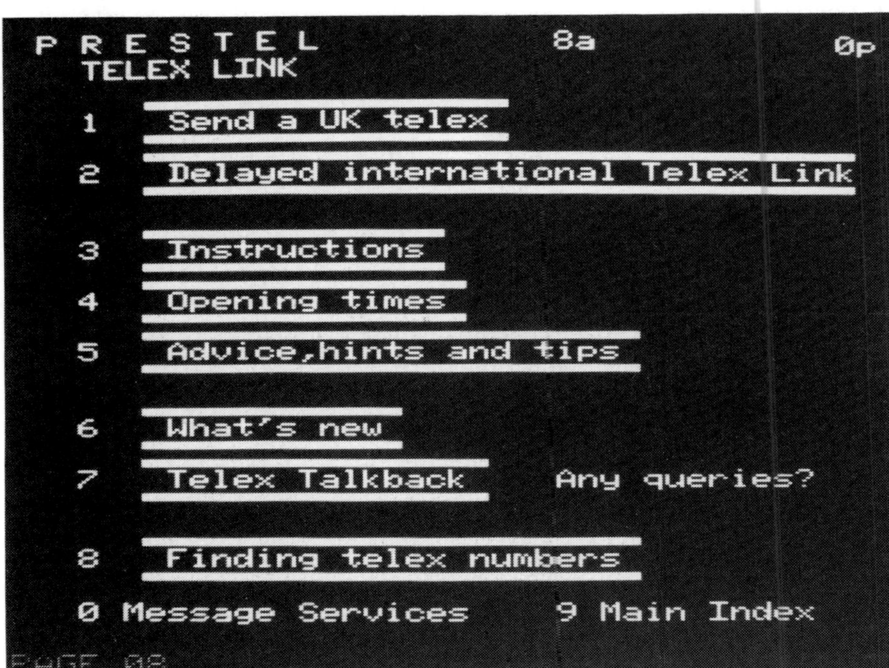

Prestel screen

kept to a minimum. As with any other telephone service, costs can be further reduced by only using the service during cheap-rate periods. The cost of any Prestel call is made up from the normal cost of the telephone call (at cheap rate where applicable), a charge per minute for accessing Prestel and an additional charge for some of the pages. You are sent a separate bill for the last two items, which also includes a quarterly charge.

Prestel pages are accessed by selecting from a sequence of menus. You can save yourself money by looking up the number of the page you want in the Prestel Directory (supplied free to users) before you start.

Some special features of Prestel include:

- *Private Pages* These are pages allocated to specialist groups of users for which you need an additional access code.
- *Mailbox* A messaging service for contacting other Prestel users.
- *Response frames* These are generally provided by commercial companies who are advertising their services. The response frame is a page at

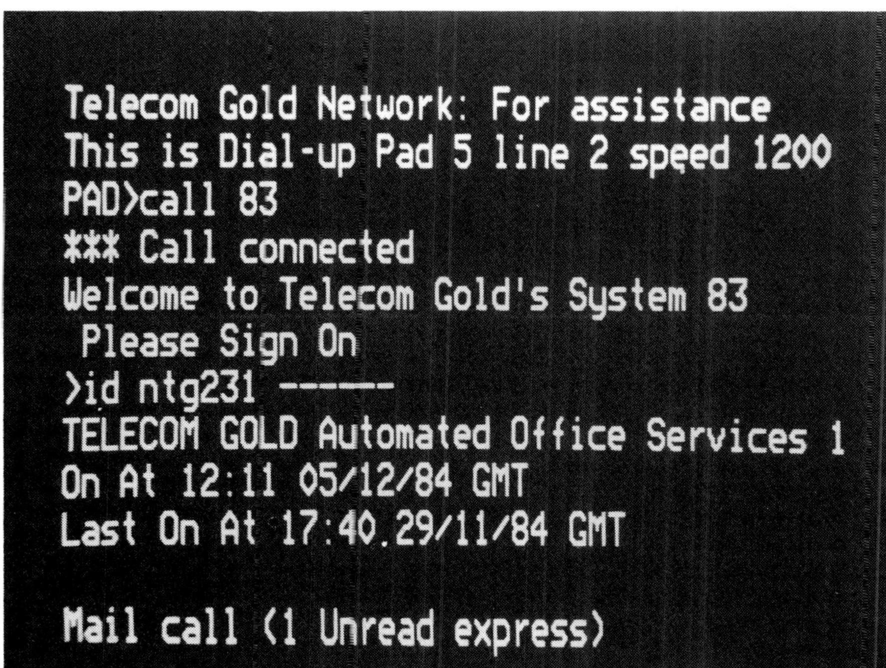

Telecom Gold screen

the end of the sequence where you can enter information to be sent to the provider of the pages (for example to order goods).

- *Gateway* It is at this stage that the sheer volume of data available becomes mind-boggling. This option literally opens up a 'gateway' to external databases linked to the Prestel system. As long as you know what you want and where to look for it you can access all types of information quickly and cheaply.

Telecom Gold provides electronic mail services and can be accessed directly by programs such as Chitchat.

A service worth considering is the Free-Phone Service, whereby your customers, or potential customers, can contact you free of charge, either by dialling the operator and asking for a Freephone number or by using the 0800 link-line prefix. BT are facing stiff competition in this from Service 800.

Communications is one area of office automation where the price, quality and variety of products is monitored and, to a certain extent, controlled. A body

The OPD/Tonto

called Oftel (the Office of Telecommunications) is charged with the task of safeguarding the interests of the consumer in this area.

The OPD/Tonto

The amalgamation of the computer and the telephone is coming closer all the time. Indeed, some machines go a long way towards it by incorporating a modem in the main system unit. The schizophrenic ICL One-Per-Desk or Merlin Tonto (one and the same machine, but sold under different names by different conglomerates), goes one step further by combining a phone and a computer in a single piece of hardware. Not only is the machine unsure of its name, it is not certain whether it is a telephone or a computer.

In fact, the two technologies fit well together and the OPD/Tonto includes an impressive collection of features: full microcomputer facilities, the four Xchange programs supplied as standard, standard telephone, automatic redial, rapid-selection directory, modem, computer access software, Messaging (optional on the Tonto but standard on the OPD, one of the few cosmetic

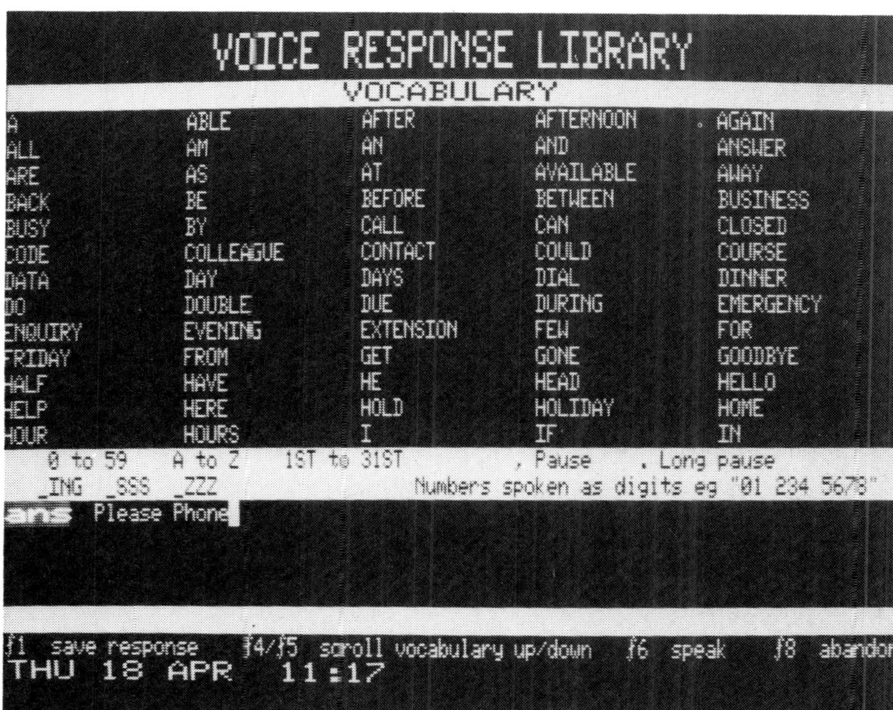

OPD/Tonto's voice response library

differences between the two), and an automatic answering machine which cannot record messages from the caller but can surprise your friends and colleagues with a stilted simulated voice message compiled from a vocabulary of over 200 words. Great fun can be had by all in constructing non-standard messages.

The main drawback in these otherwise versatile machines is their use of tiny tape cartridges for data storage. A separate disk unit can be attached, but this reduces the advantage of having all your desktop equipment in a single unit. There is no doubt that the one-stop workstation, perhaps including dictation facilities and a printer, is something we can look forward to in the not too distant future.

Chapter 11

Maintenance, training and implementation

It is when you have installed the equipment that the task of running an automated office really starts to get interesting. You have to make sure that you are not plagued by hardware failures, train those who work in the office to use the equipment, and ease the new systems into regular use. This chapter looks at the after-effects of office automation.

Maintenance

Keeping your office automation equipment in good order and active as much of the time as possible is the key to making a success of the new technologies and ensuring the maximum efficiency is achieved from their introduction.

For the first twelve months after purchase (sometimes longer) the guarantee will ensure that any problems arising from faults in the equipment itself are catered for and can be dealt with. But this does not account for problems that you create and are not covered by the guarantee (can you really blame the coffee stains inside the keyboard on faulty workmanship?). Nor does it help when the machine breaks down a year and a day after purchase.

Preventing problems

Before considering ways in which you may try to cure potential problems you should first decide what preventative measures you are going to take to avoid the problems.

There are some obvious precautions that can be taken. Dust covers are an essential way of cutting out many potential problems. Good working practices are as important as any specialist device in keeping problems down to a minimum.

Make sure that the dust covers are put on after use. Keep food and drinks well away from the working area. Store disks and other valuable media in a dust-proof container, in a safe location.

Remember that the working conditions of the people in the office are far more important than those of the machines. Those working with monitors should be given regular breaks. Plenty of space is needed as well as a light, airy office.

Coping with cables

One of the biggest problems with all this equipment is the amount of cabling that comes with it. If you're lucky there will only be one cable with each separate system. Far too many computers are still supplied with a separate plug for each individual device and this can only lead to more problems. Coping with this means making sure that you have sufficient sockets available and that they are in the right places. Make sure that your carpet does not look like an aerial view of Spaghetti Junction.

If you don't have any option over position of sockets, at least make sure that the equipment is placed as close as possible; and never allow a situation where people have to step over cables. Not only does this create a danger of someone's computer becoming accidentally unplugged, it is also a danger to your staff.

If the machines and their sockets cannot be satisfactorily matched up then it may well be worth investing in some rewiring work. Don't overload sockets; you should not have more than one item per socket if it can be avoided.

If planning a new office, make sure you plan for plenty of sockets. It is surprising how many you will need as time goes on and you should add a few more than you think you will require at the moment. Four sockets per desk is really a minimum, as well as a number of general sockets for the photocopier, radio, office kettle and so on.

Finally, you need to avoid situations where one person turns off another's computer by mistake. The chances of this will obviously be reduced by providing each desk with its own set of sockets. But it is surprising how much trouble can be avoided by simple devices such as using different coloured plugs. If all computers have green plugs while those of the printers are blue, then someone wanting to borrow your printer is unlikely to bring your current set of accounts to an untimely end.

As a final word of warning, it is always a good idea to save your work before switching off or unplugging any device. Even if you are scrupulously careful in choosing the right device, the sudden power fluctuation can, on rare occasions, cause problems with the equipment connected to neighbouring sockets.

Third-party maintenance

The answer to the problem of maintenance is sometimes to take out a third-party maintenance agreement. The number of companies specialising in the repair and servicing of our equipment is growing all the time. Some companies specialise in particular categories of equipment – for example, photocopiers and fax machines only – while others restrict their work to specific makes only.

Whether you are better to go to a large organisation with an established reputation or a smaller, local company is really a matter of personal preference and experience. Once again this is an area where you can pick up valuable tips from others using similar equipment. They may well be able to point you in the direction of a tried and trusted company.

There are many companies around at the moment that offer this type of service but some of these are now being swallowed up by the larger concerns. Whether or not this is going to be a good thing in the future is a matter for conjecture but as with everything else it is likely that there will always be a place for the small, local company, offering a fast and reliable service at a reasonable price and with a reputation built from its past success.

If you cannot find anyone to advise you on a particular company then there are a couple of pointers worth looking for. The British Standards Institute have introduced a certificate for third-party maintenance. As yet it has only been issued in the main to the larger manufacturers, such as IBM, Hewlett-Packard and Texas Instruments, companies from whom you should expect a high degree of service anyway. One non-manufacturing company that has been awarded the certificate is Bell Technical Services; this is a rapidly expanding subsidiary of a Canadian firm that offers maintenance in most levels of computer hardware.

For the smaller companies, membership of the Computing Services Association is a good indication of an effective service. The CSA has codes of conduct and sets standards which it expects its members to follow.

When selecting a maintenance company, either for a maintenace agreement or to call out in an emergency, the following points should be considered:

- *Response time* The operation of your business may depend upon getting problems sorted out quickly and effectively.
- *Hourly rate* The cost of maintenance can be very high. Some companies offer a fixed rate per hour, others charge a high call-out fee with a lower hourly charge.
- *Qualifications* Some evidence of the competence of the company will ensure that your repairs will be carried out professionally by people who know what they are doing, rather than swapping parts at random until they find the one that's causing the problem.
- *Distance to service centre* For minor problems in particular, you will not want to be too far away from the engineers. In many cases it is cheaper to take the machine in to the engineers, especially for small adjustments. You could well find that your original dealer has the facilities to offer most of the help you need, especially if you are a long way from the bases of the specialist service companies.

Getting out of difficulties

If you do not take up any sort of maintenance agreement then you should find yourself a reliable company to sort out your future problems before they arise. You can almost guarantee that something will go wrong at the most awkward moment and a great deal of time can be wasted telephoning round to try and find someone to help.

The problem will seem far less oppressive if you have the number of a suitable firm to hand and you have previously made contact with someone from that firm, so that you understand how they work, what sort of service they offer and have generally built up the basis for a good working relationship.

Most important of all, you should not attempt to carry out repairs unless you are qualified to do so. In most cases any tampering with the equipment will invalidate the guarantee.

Disk problems

If you have a problem with a damaged disk, then there are a number of possible ways of recovering from the situation:

- If you have strictly followed the back-up procedures then you can simply return to the previous copy, update it with whatever changes have been made, make a new copy and carry on.

- If this is not possible (and the problems always arise when you haven't had time to make a copy) then there are programs that will attempt to reconstruct damaged disks. Often it is possible to recover large areas of the disk and you may be able to get most of the data back, although it may be in a number of discrete blocks that have to be 'stuck' together again. One of the most famous sets of software in this category are the Norton Utilities, which provide a number of other services and are well worth the investment.

- Some computer shops offer a service to restore lost data in this way and this can be a cheap alternative, especially in relation to the value of the data on the disk. Even if you can recreate a disk from the raw data, the time taken to do so may justify the expense of bringing in outside assistance.

- If you have damaged the program disk then you can return to another copy of the original without any difficulty at all. If you didn't take a copy and have wrecked the original then there really is nothing to do except realise that you have just learnt about backups the hard way! If you are lucky your dealer may help you out, but will probably charge for the privilege, especially if it is some time since you bought the program.

- If you have a program with a built-in copy protection system that insists on the original being loaded every time you start the program then the software company should offer a service to replace damaged disks by return of post. Check up on this before you buy.

While it is very difficult to destroy a disk beyond repair it can, and frequently does, happen. For example, formatting a disk completely wipes the data surface clean and is a totally irrecoverable error.

Training

The training of individuals to look after your new equipment can vary from a five-minute session with the manual to a full ten-day residential course. The method adopted depends upon the equipment installed, its complexity of use, previous experience and the potential cost of major mistakes.

For something like a photocopier or facsimile machine, the dealer or installation engineer should be able to show you very quickly how to operate the equipment at its most basic level. The more sophisticated features can be investigated by dipping into the manual, followed by a little bit of trial and error. In the end most of the procedures that are regularly needed can be learnt by experience.

With any new equipment or software, if you are familiar with one model or version the transition to a new one should not be too traumatic.

Learning to use a computer or word processor for the first time is a very different matter. Even with extensive training the system is not going to be mastered in a day and you should prepare yourself for a prolonged period of learning before the system begins to be used at its most efficient.

The manual for any item of hardware or software should tell you all you need to know in order to complete the installation and get it up and running. It should also provide you with the basics of operation of the system and give a complete summary of its capabilities. However it cannot be expected to give you full qualifications in the topic.

For example, a word-processor program manual should tell you how to make copies of the disks, how to start the program and give a simple guide to entering text and storing it away on disk. Editing procedures should also be covered as well as a description of each of the commands. The reference section should list all commands and features of the program. You will be extremely lucky if the manual gives instruction on how to produce the most effective layout or precise details of how to get special effects using the printer.

This sort of detail can only be learnt through experience or by attending a course of some sort. Certainly for any complex new system, if no-one is available with sufficient knowledge to pass on to others, then it is certainly well worthwhile sending one member of staff at least on some sort of course in order to speed up the process. Learning by mistakes is all very well, but in a busy office there is often just not the time for this sort of luxury and some mistakes can be very costly indeed. Organised training may seem expensive but put in the context of wasted time and resources it frequently works out as a very cheap option.

The person who is trained in this way is then in a position to pass on what they have learned to others. It is important to realise, though, that one course does not provide all the experience that is needed to make a success of the system. No matter how intensive the course may be it will only ever provide the foundations of knowledge that can be built on with experience to create a full, working understanding of the system and its concepts.

Many of the more expensive programs – especially those that have been written for a specific industry or are designed to meet the needs of a particular customer – will include an element of training within the price. This may include a half-day spent setting up the system and initiating the user in its operation, it may be a full training seminar or it may simply consist of a cassette tape.

If none of these is provided then you will have to look outside. The availability of a suitable course or someone who is prepared to instruct you is often a factor in deciding which product to buy.

The courses you find may be quite general and not specific to one program or another; however most programs operate on broadly similar principles and once you have mastered the main concepts involved it is a relatively straightforward matter to transfer to another, similar package.

Audio cassettes have become quite popular over the last few years as a training medium. There is no doubt that they do have a number of major benefits. You can learn at your own pace and in your own time. If you did not fully understand a section then it can be replayed.

The main disadvantage is that this is very much a one-way system. There is no interaction between the pupil and the tape. If there is something you do not understand or a section you would like explained in more detail then you cannot ask questions or get any sort of feedback. In such cases you are left to work it out for yourself.

An extension of this medium but with the ability to respond to the user's input is interactive video. The path taken by the course here depends upon the responses of the user and the course is programmed to react according to the results that are fed into it. However, this form of training is still at a very early stage of development and cannot be considered a universally available and viable alternative for some time to come.

Many manufacturers provide free tutorials on disk that take you through the basics of the program. You can also buy tutorials from independent suppliers; these are generally more detailed and of a higher quality but you should check them out fairly carefully before you buy to make sure they are aimed at the level of training you require.

This also applies to courses; it is no good booking up for a beginner's course if you already know the basics but an advanced course will be a waste of money if you have not grasped the fundamentals of the topic.

Implementation

The way in which any new system is introduced into the office is of crucial importance to its acceptance and therefore its success. It is important to have a full plan of implementation and to allow sufficient time for the development of staff skills. In particular you must make allowances for time for training, whatever form that may take.

The planned introduction

If you have decided to go in for office automation in a big way, then do not expect to change everything overnight. New systems should be introduced gradually and not all at once. Any new product is bound to create teething problems; things never go quite as smoothly as one would hope.

In an ideal world any new development would be set aside in a corner somewhere until everyone had had sufficient time to familiarise themselves with it, at which stage it could come on-stream and begin to contribute to office life. In most busy offices this gentle approach is simply just not viable and the new product is expected to start paying for itself straight away.

As well as all the normal difficulties of everyday office life you also have to cope with the problems created by the new system and the fact that other people are short of time because of your training program. Rushing into a number of new systems at once is therefore likely to lead to these problems being compounded and the whole office grinding to a halt, not quite what was originally intended!

The great danger is that those who have to work with the system just do not have the time to give it a fair trial. In such circumstances they can declare that the system is obviously totally unsuited to their working practices and refuse to go any further with it. The result is that they go back to the old ways to 'sort out the mess', the system is relegated to the broom cupboard and is never seen again.

Surprisingly, this sort of occurrence is not as scarce as one might think. A great deal of money is spent on office automation each year; if any calculations were done of how much of that money was completely wasted it would be a frighteningly high proportion.

Phased introduction and tandem systems

You need to have faith in any new system that is introduced but not blind faith. Where possible a system should be totally tested before it is trusted with full responsibility for some part of your operation. Before you fully commit yourself to any major new project you need to be sure that the system can respond in the way you require.

This is just as true of the new facsimile machine as the stock control program. Don't offer a bureau service for sending messages around the world until you are satisfied that you are competent enough to complete the process without looking foolish in front of any customers who may wander in to take advantage of the new service you are offering.

In the case of a computer system, such as an accounts package, you should try to run the new system in tandem with your old manual methods, for a time at least. This is time-consuming in the initial stages, but in the end it will pay off.

If you are confident that any errors that might occur can be corrected then the introduction of the system is going to save a great amount of worry. Knowing that you can always compare the old with the new to find out if everything is alright and, if not, where it has gone wrong, results in less sleepless nights and fewer frayed tempers. This in itself will cut down on further mistakes. Working under pressure with a system you don't understand invariably leads to a sense of panic that can completely disrupt any activity.

Keeping your enthusiasm under control

It is sometimes said that the job of the manager in charge of office automation is to keep in touch with all new developments. Often this is the last thing you want to do! As described in an earlier chapter, enviously scanning the trade press for the latest developments can make your system look antique even before the guarantee has run out.

The same applies to all the little 'additions' that are constantly being praised up in the advertisements and in the press. There is a great deal of money to be made out of servicing the new technology; many of the products around are absolutely essential but likewise many of them are totally dispensible luxuries.

You cannot run a microcomputer without floppy disks, for example, and it is well worth spending a little more on disks that you know will be reliable. But do you really need to invest in a special pen for writing disk labels, whose point will break off if you exert too much pressure? Surely it is far better to impress upon your staff the need to write the labels *before* they are stuck on the disks and invest a few pence in a few extra labels for those occasions when you re-use a disk (or better still, a cheap felt-tip pen)?

Reading up on other gadgets can also induce a state of panic that is often totally unwarranted. The problem of fluctuations in the mains power supply is not one that is going to worry most computer users. Very rarely a power surge may cause your computer to crash but once again the cheap, simple and effective answer is to train yourself and others to permanently save what they are doing, regularly and often. It is only necessary to invest in an expensive device to smooth out mains 'spikes' if you have already ascertained that there really is a problem.

Similarly, a great deal of fear is induced on the subject of static, resulting in the purchase of a range of products, from special mats to aerosol sprays. Being told that walking around your desk for ten seconds can give you a charge of 30,000 volts is quite a terrifying prospect. However, few people seem to suffer static problems and it really comes down to a question of identifying the real scale of the problem before you start investing large amounts in the solutions. Computer paranoia is becoming increasingly prevalent!

On the other hand, a little wise expenditure at an early stage can save a hefty bill to put right avoidable problems. Most equipment is impaired by excessive amounts of dust and this inevitably leads to difficulties. If a keyboard starts to play up it can often be that it is simply clogged up with dirt; getting it properly and professionally cleaned is then a necessary expense but one that could have been avoided by the use of a dust cover. This does not need to be an expensive item – all it has to do is cover the machine – so something cheap will do. It doesn't matter if it doesn't look very smart as long as it does the job.

Basically it comes down to common sense. Don't get carried away and don't panic. Of course, you should have an eye to the future and keep abreast of new developments so that you can plan how best to upgrade your systems when the time comes but only if you can be certain that it will not lead to dissatisfaction with what you already have and a rush into something more advanced before the present system has outlived its usefulness.

Health and Safety

As the manager of an automated office you are also responsible for safety, comfort and general well-being of those who work in the office.

Although there have been various scare stories about the dangers of constant working in front of a visual display unit (monitor) most authorities now agree that these worries are unfounded. However, long periods in front of the screen can certainly be stressful and anyone working at a computer for long periods should be entitled to frequent breaks.

Design of the seating and height and position of the desktop are also crucial to the comfort of the operators and the avoidance of health problems caused by awkward working conditions.

Noise is also an important factor and great improvements can be effected at relatively low cost by the use of accoustic heads for printers.

Work areas should be well lit and air conditioning helps maintain an even temperature and provides fresh air, which are important to both operator and machine alike.

Summary

So, to ensure a smooth lead-in to any new system:

- Only introduce as few new elements at a time as possible.
- Set aside time for training and plan for longer times than normal to get the same results.
- Introduce the new system in tandem with the old, maintaining the two until you are satisfied that you have the new system fully under control.
- Don't get carried away by the technology; you may not be aiming to save money but you can avoid wasting it.
- Make sure that you pay as much attention to the people who have to work in the office as you do to the machines they operate.

Chapter 12

Final considerations

Any manager needs to be aware of his legal responsibilities so this chapter provides a brief introduction to the important Data Protection Act. Following this some further sources of information are indicated.

The Data Protection Act

Any new or existing computer user should be aware of the regulations laid down by the 1984 Data Protection Act. This Act aims to control the use of any automatically processed information that relates to individuals. It also enshrines in law the rights of the individual with relation to any data held about him or her.

The Act is specifically aimed at *personal data*, which is broadly defined as information about a living individual, including expressions of opinion about him or her. However, the Act excludes from this description any information that gives an indication of the intentions of the 'Data User' with respect to that individual.

There are certain exceptions relating to data held for recreational purpose, data used solely for business accounts and data that the user is required by law to make public; there are also a number of other limitated exemptions as well as a wealth of grey areas.

Anyone who stores, or intends to store, such personal data on a computer is required by law to register. Those registering will come under one of the headings:

- *Data users* These are individual companies or organisations who control or process personal data on a computer (or other automated processor).

- *Computer bureaux* This rather loose term includes anyone who processes another user's personal data. Thus if your equipment is used to provide a service to someone else that includes the processing of personal data you are obliged to register as a Computer Bureau even though you do not trade as such.

Essentially, if you think you may store anything that might be considered as personal data you are obliged to at least make enquiries of the Data Protection Register to see if your circumstances compel you to be registered.

On registration the following information must be supplied:

- The form of the personal data.

- The uses to which the data is to be put.

- The source of the data.

- Those to whom the data may be disclosed.

- Any countries outside the UK where the data may be transferred.

A registered user has certain responsibilities:

- The data must be collected fairly and lawfully.

- The data can only be used for registered purposes and must be relevant to those purposes.

- Only registered recipients may receive the data and the data must be secure against unauthorised access.

- The data must be accurate, up-to-date and held only for as long as is necessary.

Anyone whose personal data is held or processed by computer also has a number of new rights:

- An individual can ask a Data User whether he holds personal data and, if so, can ask for a copy of the relevant data. The User may charge a few pounds and is obliged to verify the identity of the person making the request. Repeated request can only be made at 'reasonable intervals'.

- Any inaccuracies discovered in the data must be rectified. If necessary the individual can get a Court order to correct or erase the false data.

- Courts can award compensation for damage or distress suffered by the individual as a result of the loss of data, inaccurate or misleading data, or the disclosure of data to an unauthorised person; the compensation is only payable if the User cannot prove that reasonable care was taken in the collection and processing of the data.

This Act, though long overdue, opens up a minefield of areas where problems may arise. Although providing essential safeguards for the individual it can also work against the individual; until the processing of manual data is properly covered by the legislation much contentious information can still be processed in other ways or may have an adverse effect on the individual even though it doesn't actually appear in permanent form.

The Act also provides safeguards for the User and is therefore a very good step in the right direction. Experience from both this country and abroad will no doubt lead to more watertight and clearly defined legislation. The important thing for the office manager is to be aware of the legislation and his responsibility to register.

Other sources of information

The world is awash with information, especially when it comes to information about office automation. If you require further information on any particular aspect of the subject there are a number of sources to which you can turn:

- *Books* There are many books available, from general books (such as this one) to books covering a special area of interest, such as a particular machine or range of software.

- *Magazines* The number of specialist magazines continues to increase. These range from general magazines such as *Personal Computer World (PCW)*, to those for specific computers, e.g. *Amstrad User*. Some are highly technical and aimed at the experienced user.

- *Free magazines* A visit to a computer show guarantees a flood of free magazines regularly dropping onto the office mat (especially if you fill out the little cards that are thrust at you at various stands). These magazines derive their revenues almost solely from advertising and therefore rely upon high circulation figures. It is normal to have to re-register after three years in order to satisfy the rules of the Audit Bureau of Circulation.

Some of these have a newspaper format; often these relate more closely to users of mainframe computers. Others have a more glossy format and relate either to microcomputers, e.g. *PC Magazine* for IBM-compatibles or business in general (*Mind Your Own Business* being an excellent example).

A few claim to have a subscription rate and ask for a subscription after a few free issues have been sent. In some cases the free issues stop if no subscription is forthcoming.

Generally, the quality is high and the information supplied is accurate and up-to-date.

- *Consultants* Although paying for advice seems expensive it can save a great deal of money in the long run, and the assistance of a well-established independent consultant can pay great dividends.

- *National Computing Centre* This is a Government-sponsored organisation that has computer centres at a number of locations around the country. The centres provide advice, hands-on experience of equipment and consultancy. Some of their services are free, for others a charge is levied.

- *User groups* The user groups for a particular machine can be an invaluable source of information, since they will keep you up to date on new equipment and features, modifications, new software and so on. They will also provide news of problems that have been discovered with hardware or software and explain how to overcome and avoid these. If you take up their offers of software and other products at a discounted price the subscription soon pays for itself.

  Often there is more than one user group; as well as a group organised by the manufacturer there may be independent groups who take a more critical view of the manufacturer's activities and the performance of his products.

- *Bulletin boards* One of the most interesting ways of gaining information – if you have the time to spare – is through the medium of bulletin boards. These are information centres that can be accessed by your computer over the telephone lines.

Other sources of information include existing users, professional organisations (who can give you help with automation of your own particular profession) and dealers. The important thing is to make sure you get a good range of views before you make any important decision. Take with a pinch of salt anyone who is obsessively in favour of or against a particular product, any enthusiast who uses a machine 'for fun' or a dealer or consultant who sells the product for profit or gets commission by recommending it.

Of course, it is sometimes difficult to distinguish between the dealer who recommends a product because he gets commission and the one who chooses to deal with a product because he knows it is good. Very few products are all bad and none is perfect, so the 'four legs good, two legs bad' response needs to be regarded with more than a little scepticism.

By careful consideration of the merits of various types of equipment, by comparisons of costs and estimated savings, and by a realistic appraisal of the real needs of the office it should be possible to devise an office automation scheme that will enhance your service to customers, improve the working conditions of staff and gerally make working in the office in future a more enjoyable experience. There is no doubt that in a few years time our office working practices will bear little resemblance to those we have now but the coming years are surely going to be an exciting, challenging and rewarding time.

Index